Evolving English WordBank

a glossary of present-day English dialect and slang

Jonathan Robinson

BRADWELL
BOOKS

Published by Bradwell Books

9 Orgreave Close Sheffield S13 9NP

Email: books@bradwellbooks.co.uk

© Jonathan Robinson 2015

British Library Cataloguing in Publication Data: a catalogue record for this book is available from the British Library.

1st Edition

Hardback ISBN: 9781909914896

Print: Gomer Press, Llandysul, Ceredigion SA44 4JL

Design by: Mark Titterton

Cover Design by: Andrew Caffrey

Photograph Credits: IStock

Dedication

To Al for being *me duck*; my dad for having a distinctive *peff*; my *mom* for holding my *donny*; and Ben, Ellie and Ami for playing *forty forty* in the garden at Lockslea where Andrew, Helen and I played *acky one two three*.

Jonathan Robinson November 2014

EVOLVING *ENGLISH* WORDBANK

A GLOSSARY OF PRESENT-DAY ENGLISH DIALECT AND SLANG

Jonathan Robinson

BRADWELL
BOOKS

Foreword

The British Library's 2010 exhibition 'Evolving English: One Language, Many Voices', on which this book is based, is the most popular winter exhibition that the Library has ever held. That a major component of the exhibition, as Jonnie Robinson explains, was public participation in recording everyday speech and commenting on local words is testimony to the Library's vision in seeing the importance of vigorous non-standard language to the health of the language as a whole. Setting this project at the exhibition alongside the displaying of such treasures as the original manuscript of *Beowulf* firmly underlined the message. All too often users of non-standard English have been made to think of their speech as inferior, to believe their inherited local words, grammar and pronunciation fall short of some notional ideal. The 2010 exhibition did much to dispel myths surrounding local variety, removing it from the shackles of prescriptivism and grounding it in the history and culture of Britain.

From the outset, this splendid book grips readers with the essentials of the study of language varieties. There is plenty for everyone, however expert they might think themselves to be, but anyone coming to the study of the non-standard language for the first time will, having read the introductory explanations, be in possession of all they need properly to understand the subject. They will indeed be disabused of misconceptions, such as those surrounding what comprises 'dialect' and separates it from 'slang', held by some supposed expert linguists. Yet it is a measure of the author's consummate grasp of his subject that all this is done with the lightest of touches.

Thus prepared, readers can go on confidently to confront selected gems from the WordBank that emerged from 'Evolving English'. That vernacular speech is firmly grounded in the history of English is constantly in view: visit *howfing*, *oxter*, and *twitchel* for immediate proof. (I myself am delighted to see that my *pikelet* really was a word for (Standard) 'crumpet' as far back as the eighteenth century.) And that non-standard invention remains popular today is clear: go straight to *banterous*, *deaf* and *LMAO* for proof of this. The extended notes accompanying many of the WordBank entries take the user well beyond the confines of the word or phrase itself, providing insight into the way in which an enthusiastic enquirer can branch out from one word in a host of directions. And, should the reader be inspired to go on their own voyages of discovery, the concluding section on 'Dialect collectors' shows the way.

Only Jonnie Robinson could have produced this book. With a formal academic grounding in dialectology and sociolinguistics, the compendious web-based presentation of the British Library's vernacular speech holdings to his credit, and the distinction of co-curating the phenomenon that was the 'Evolving English' exhibition, this is his subject. The user of this book travels with the best of guides.

Clive Upton

Emeritus Professor of Modern English Language, University of Leeds

Introduction

Mam's the word

'Me mam' – it means 'your mum' or summat like that.

These are the words of a twelve-year-old girl from Hull recorded at the British Library's 'Evolving English' exhibition in 2010. 'Evolving English: One Language, Many Voices' was a major exhibition that explored the evolution of the English language over 1,500 years through the Library's extensive collection of manuscripts, printed books, newspapers, sound recordings, digital media and ephemera. The exhibition celebrated historic and contemporary diversity by presenting examples of English usage across time and space. Visitors to the Library's Paccar Gallery in St Pancras and to complementary mini exhibitions held at six partner libraries across England (Birmingham, Leeds, Liverpool, Newcastle, Norwich and Plymouth) were encouraged to contribute a voice recording to create a snapshot of spoken English at the start of the 21st century. They could either submit a word or phrase they felt was somehow 'special' in their variety of English (the 'WordBank') or recite a reading passage designed to capture their accent (the 'VoiceBank').

The public and media response to the exhibition confirmed enormous enthusiasm for debate about many aspects of the English language, but above all demonstrated our fascination with, and affection for, features of English with which we connect on a personal level – the dialects, accents, slang and nonce-words that express our sense of individual and shared identities. The exhibition attracted over 147,000 visitors, approximately 15,000 of whom – such as the contributor from Hull – submitted recordings that resulted in a substantial audio archive. As with previous attempts to collect vernacular English, the WordBank shows what our everyday vocabulary reveals about our identities – a speaker's preference for *aged P*, *bibi*, *M*, *ma*, *mam*, *mamma*, *marge*, *marmie*, *mater*, *mom*, *mother*, *mum*, *muma*, *mummy*, *mummy-ji*, *muv* or *old dear* for 'female parent' gives subtle clues about social status, gender, ethnicity, geographic background and/or age. This book celebrates such present-day English lexical variation by presenting selected items from the WordBank.

Lexical variation

We can observe lexical variation by comparing the way English is spoken in different places and among different social groups. All languages change over time and vary according to place and social setting and the words we use are influenced by many factors – family heritage, social and educational background, environment, friends, audience, purpose and, equally importantly, our own sense of identity. All native speakers also adjust their speech according to context: from relaxed conversation in familiar surroundings to more formal situations so we have a range of words for expressing the same notion. Most of us, for instance, avoid saying *knackered* [= 'tired'] when speaking to young children or foreigners, but use it without hesitation among friends. Individuals vary as to whether they use *knackered* in the presence of older family members or superiors at work, perhaps preferring more mainstream colloquial variants like *shattered, done in* or *bushed*. And then there are other terms like *jiggered, wabbit* or *cream-crackered* that tend to occur among speakers who share a common regional background. In most cases the choices we make are subconscious, but they nevertheless express a shared identity, reinforce group solidarity or present a certain image.

Dialect

The terms dialect, accent and slang are often used interchangeably, although in strict linguistic terms they refer to different aspects of language variation. A dialect is a variety of English that differs from other varieties in three key ways: lexis (vocabulary), phonology (pronunciation) and grammar (structure). English dialects may be distinct from each other, but all speakers within the English-speaking world can still generally understand them. Some speakers from Sheffield, for instance, might pepper their speech with localised vocabulary, such as *mardy* [= 'moody, sulky, spoilt'] or *nowt* [= 'nothing'] and/or use non-standard grammatical constructions, such as singular object *us* [= 'me'] and possessive *me* [= 'my'], as in *can you pass us me coat*. Such speakers inevitably also use local pronunciations so can legitimately be described as Sheffield dialect speakers. Despite the popular belief that dialect words in particular are no longer very widely used, there remains a great deal of lexical diversity in the UK.

Accent

Accent, on the other hand, refers only to the sound patterns of a specific dialect. The word *nothing*, for instance, can be pronounced in several ways: some speakers consistently pronounce the final syllable <-ing> to rhyme with 'thing', others invariably pronounce it to rhyme with 'thin' while many of us use both pronunciations – the former in formal speech and the latter in informal contexts. In an area centred on Birmingham, Manchester and Liverpool many speakers pronounce the word final <g>, particularly if *nothing* is followed by a vowel in collocations such as *nothing at all*, while a pronunciation with a word final <k> (i.e. rhyming with 'think') is common across the country. In some places – notably in East Anglia and Newcastle upon Tyne – the final syllable is often pronounced with a comparatively weak vowel, similar to the final <-en> in the word *listen*. The pronunciation of the vowel in the first syllable <noth-> can be even more revealing about a speaker's geographic background. Speakers in the north of England vary between an <o> sound (i.e. to rhyme with 'goth') or with a 'northern' <u> sound – often represented in popular descriptions as if it were spelt 'noothing'. In the south of England a 'southern' <u> sound is most common (i.e. as if it were 'nuhthing'), although in broad local speech in the south east this can seem quite close to an <a> sound (i.e. as if it were 'nathing'). Finally the word medial <-th-> sound can also vary: a stereotypical London pronunciation is often represented as 'naffin', while some speakers in Liverpool might say something that sounds to outsiders a little like 'not'n'.

In several dialects in the north of England, some speakers use *nowt* as a variant of *nothing*, but this, too, is pronounced differently according to location. In Middlesbrough, for instance, it is generally pronounced to rhyme with 'out', while in Sheffield it usually sounds more like 'oat'. Sheffield-born lead singer of Arctic Monkeys, Alex Turner, pronounces it this way when singing the line *he makes examples of you and there's nowt you can say* in 'From the Ritz to the Rubble', a 2006 song which contains several dialect forms and – unusually for a commercial rock song – is sung in a Sheffield accent. In the opening verse, for instance, Turner rhymes *totalitarian* with *scary one* [pronounced 'scary 'un'] and sings *you can swap jumpers and make* [pronounced 'meck'] *another move*. In reality the majority of speakers from Sheffield use predominantly mainstream vocabulary and grammar, but their pronunciation is nonetheless distinctly local. Such speakers should properly be described as having a Sheffield accent. In other words, dialect is an umbrella term for a variety of linguistic features, of which one is accent. True dialect speakers are arguably relatively rare in some parts of the UK, but despite popular belief we all speak with an accent.

Slang

Vocabulary restricted to use among speakers with a common experience, interest or lifestyle is properly described as either jargon or slang. The dividing line between the two is not always clear-cut but strictly speaking jargon refers to specialised vocabulary used, for instance, by people in the same occupation or profession or with shared hobbies. Football jargon includes terms like *nutmeg* [= 'to play the ball through the legs of an opponent'], *woodwork* [= 'goalposts and crossbar'] and *Derby* [= 'match between two local rival teams']. Although perhaps not immediately comprehensible all three are conventional terms used in rule books, coaching manuals, matchday programmes, magazines, press reports, broadcast coverage and by players and fans. Slang, in contrast, is used to reinforce relationships or affirm solidarity among speakers or can be used deliberately to create barriers between speakers. Many footballers and football fans, for example, talk disapprovingly of teams *parking the bus* [= 'adopting an ultra-defensive formation to prevent the opposition scoring'], dismiss mild confrontations or scuffles between opposing players as *handbags* and during an impromptu kick-about with friends might suggest *rush goalies* [= 'agreement in small-sided game that any player nearest goal may act as goalkeeper']. Such terms occur regularly among footballers as a playful expression of their enthusiasm for the game, but equally importantly, as validation of their membership of an in-group of football aficionados. In other words slang is used to construct an identity, affirm a particular expertise or attitude and also as a means of excluding the uninitiated: well-known varieties such as military slang, teenspeak, Cockney rhyming slang and polari (gay slang) are – often intentionally – incomprehensible to outsiders. Some slang terms, such as *naff* [= 'useless, unfashionable, poor quality'], may eventually enter the mainstream as a colloquial term, but many are transient, swiftly replaced by newer, more fashionable terms, or are only understood by speakers of a specific clique, group or subculture. Embraced by many, ridiculed by some, slang is used by most of us in one form or another.

Nonce-words

Finally we all occasionally coin a word for an action, object or phenomenon for which no conventional term readily springs to mind. This linguistic creativity can be intentional – e.g. an original form or playful adaptation of an existing word to capture a concept more precisely or more amusingly – or accidental – e.g. a slip of the tongue or infantile pronunciation or construction. A typical feature of young children's speech, for instance, is the use of idiosyncratic expressions that communicate a notion perfectly and are often grammatically acceptable, but do not reflect idiomatic usage. The effect is often comical to adults and most families can list examples of expressions that subsequently become part of a family's repertoire. Examples within our family include the nouns *toastwich* [= 'toasted sandwich'] and *shoddies* [= 'sausages'], the adjective *blodgy* [= used negatively of jam 'with bits'], and the verbs *flimse* [= 'to break off too easily, to fall apart too readily'] and *snurk* [= 'to swap seats between main course and afters']. Strictly speaking a nonce-word is used on one occasion only, but some persist within a family or among a group of close friends. In exceptional circumstances, especially words coined by authors or famous people, they can become more widely used, such as Lewis Carroll's *chortle* and J.K. Rowling's *muggle*.

Categorising lexical items

Having sought to establish the difference between dialect (i.e. geographically specific) and slang (i.e. socially specific) vocabulary, in fact the boundary between the two is often blurred. Take the word *vexed* [= 'annoyed'], for instance. This word prompted strikingly different reactions among contributors to the BBC Voices Recordings, a set of group conversations recorded across the UK by BBC Local and Nations Radio in 2004/5 in which participants were asked to discuss the words they used for a set of everyday concepts. A group of *Evening Standard* sellers recorded in London categorise it as 'posh', while a Castleford teenager associates it with her grandfather. In contrast, British Jamaicans living in Handsworth offer it as their default term and explain they often abbreviate it to *vex* – reflecting the tendency among speakers of Caribbean varieties of English to simplify word final consonant clusters. To complicate matters further, two Bury teenagers comment that *vex*(*ed*) is widely used in rap lyrics, so they have started using it with friends. Clearly then we could legitimately classify 'vexed' as a socially prestigious form, an archaic northern dialect word, an example of Caribbean patwa, or contemporary urban slang. In fact it is all of the above depending on who uses it to whom, when and where. These multiple layers reveal the subtle nuances conveyed by an individual word or linguistic feature: at one time *vexed* enjoyed much wider currency in the UK, but over time it has evidently become restricted to certain speaker groups, while in the Caribbean it remains a mainstream form. More recently it has re-emerged in the UK among young speakers in urban centres, presumably as a result of contact with British Caribbean communities. Camden-born rapper Dappy captures this latest manifestation in the line *you don't wanna see I vex* in the 2008 song, 'Defeat You', by British hip-hop group N-Dubz.

Dialect boundaries

It is equally important to stress that very few words exist in a single geographic location. Although we all occasionally feel a sense of 'ownership' over a word we think belongs exclusively to our village, town or area this is rarely the case. One illuminating example I encountered during recent research is the term *poppy-show* [= 'show-off', 'bighead'], supplied by speakers in a BBC Voices Recording in Huddersfield as a stereotypically Jamaican patwa term. Although this is confirmed by an entry in *The Dictionary of Caribbean English Usage*, it is also recorded in *Like Dew Before the Sun: Life and Language in Northamptonshire*, a nostalgic homage to an apparently lost way of life (and speech) in rural middle England. When I first became interested in dialectology I was hopeful I might be able to plot an isogloss – a boundary on a map that separates two linguistic variants – running east–west across England and dividing speakers (I presumed in the north) who use *chuffing* as a mild profanity or euphemism and southerners who (according to my observations) use *naffing* for the same purpose. I hoped *The New Partridge Dictionary of Slang and Unconventional English* might confirm my suspicions and sure enough the respective entries include the following citations:

Dave are you gonna play the prince in the chuffin' tower all day or what? (from 1987 British film *The Full Monty* set in Sheffield)

And do you think I'd repay that by stealing your tin of naffing pineapple chunks … not even me favourite fruit (from a 1976 episode of BBC TV series *Porridge* delivered by Godber, a character from Birmingham)

However, closer inspection shows that the real picture is more complex as the *Oxford English Dictionary* also includes the following entry:

Well which one of them's got the naffing engagement ring? (from Keith Waterhouse's 1959 novel *Billy Liar*, set in the fictional town of Stradhoughton, Yorkshire)

WordBank

The Evolving English WordBank is testament to this multidimensional diversity and, moreover, proof of enormous popular interest in the English language. Contributions were made by speakers aged between six and ninety from a variety of social and geographic backgrounds across the UK, making it a uniquely inclusive and wide-ranging archive of spoken words and phrases. Compiling a small selection has been both pleasurable and enlightening. I have regularly smirked, winced and raised a quizzical eye in reacquainting myself with familiar favourites, encountering amusing banter, discovering terms I was previously unaware of and marvelling at originality and inventiveness. The WordBank is a rich resource for academic linguists that offers a variety of research enquiries, from dialectology to lexicography, but is above all a treasure trove for enthusiasts of the English language.

Although not a comprehensive record of the entire WordBank data set, the following glossary provides a snapshot of British vernacular English at the start of the 21st century, chosen to give a sense of variation according to a range of geographical and social factors. I am delighted to report, for instance, that historic local forms such as *jiffle* [= 'to fidget, wriggle about'] and *puggle* [= 'to prod, poke about in e.g. hole to clear obstruction'] – both contributed by young speakers from the south of England, where the apparent demise of local dialect is most frequently asserted – prove our regional dialects remain robust. Conversely, forms like *bubbe* [= 'grandmother'] and *thanda* [= 'cold'] reveal the influence of successive waves of migration to the UK by speakers of heritage languages from all four corners of the world, thereby enriching our language and ensuring its continued diversity. Inspired neologisms like *ding* [= 'to microwave'] and *squirgle* [= 'sausage'] bear witness to our linguistic playfulness and sheer love of the sounds of words, while fashionable terms such as *mint* [= 'great, excellent'] and *buff* [= 'attractive'] reflect our desire to identify linguistically with our peers. Above all the detailed observations provided by so many speakers clearly demonstrate the importance we attach to certain words and the affection we feel for phrases and expressions that convey a sense of self, location, friendship or family bonds.

Entries in the glossary are presented alphabetically and each item is explained in the words of the contributor(s). Some items feature multiple definitions that reveal subtle distinctions between speakers. Entries are cross-referenced, where possible, to supporting evidence and in some cases include additional editorial comment and reflection. Despite the caveat noted above about the danger of labelling words too rigidly, including a reference to an authoritative source at least hints at previous scholarly classification and thus gives a sense of a word's provenance and distribution. Many of the words occur in multiple sources, but in most cases only one is included here as a guide. Details of reference works consulted are given in table 2 below and a review of dictionaries, dialect surveys and significant attempts to collect vernacular English are given in the final section of the book.

Table 1: Key to lexical entries

1. WORD part of speech definition
 e.g. **MARDY adj.** moody, sullen, spoilt (esp. of child)

2. Speaker location (gender, year of birth, British Library catalogue ref.) *contribution in own words*
e.g. **Ashby-de-la-Zouch** (male, 1986, C1442/01473): *being grumpy and grouchy but more stroppy than that like a four-year-old throwing a paddy and mardy weather is overcast cold and rainy*

Burton upon Trent (male, 1946, C1442/00343): *an adjective I used as a boy and I don't hear anywhere else but in the East Midlands mardy refers to a boy who's being miserable and whining someone for example who would take his cricket set home 'cause he didn't want to play any more*

3. PREVIOUS EVIDENCE (date) note re: distribution/origin

e.g. **OED** (1874) 'regional, chiefly north'

4. RELATED ENTRY [where applicable]

e.g. cf. **CARNAPTIOUS**, **MAUNGY**

5. EDITORIAL NOTE [selected entries only]

e.g. NOTES The sheer number of contributors who wanted to ensure *mardy* was included in the **WordBank** testifies to the continued vitality of this much-loved dialect term. Several contributors claimed it is exclusively a Leicester word or only used in Nottingham, but it clearly occurs over a wide area of the North and Midlands, and is particularly well established in the East Midlands. DH Lawrence refers to a *mard-arsed kid* in his 1928 poem 'The Collier's Wife' and *mardy* crops up frequently in Alan Sillitoe's 1958 novel 'Saturday Night and Sunday Morning', set in Nottingham. Perhaps more impressively you now hear youngsters all over the world singing along to Arctic Monkeys' 2004 single 'Mardy Bum', meaning this nineteenth-century Midlands dialect word now enjoys international currency.

Table 2: Order in which dictionaries & survey sources were consulted

OED – Oxford English Dictionary (online)

EDD – English Dialect Dictionary (1898-1905)

DSL – Dictionary of Scots Language (online)

SED – Survey of English Dialects (1962-1971)

NPD – New Partridge Dictionary of Slang and Unconventional English (2013)

GDS – Green's Dictionary of Slang (2010)

DCS – Dictionary of Contemporary Slang (2014)

UD – Urban Dictionary (online)

KTL – Kitchen Table Lingo (2008)

VOICES – BBC Voices Recordings (2004-2005)

A

ACH-Y-FI excl. phrase used to express disgust or abhorrence

England (female, C1442/02622) *my dad uses the word ach-y-fi but that's actually Welsh it means dirty pig he used it to describe my brother I grew up in England so I would never use it outside my family but we find it amusing*

Collins English Dictionary 'Welsh' *ach, achy* [= exclamation of disgust] + *fi* [= 'I, me']

AGGY adj. aggressive, argumentative, confrontational

East London (female, 1993, C1442/00535) *aggy it doesn't really mean angry if you describe someone as being aggy then it's because they're being aggressive and rude*

UD (2004)

ALL MY EYE AND BETTY MARTIN excl. phrase used to express disbelief, surprise or denial

Wales (female, 1947, C1442/02687) *I use the phrase all my eye and Betty Martin which my mother used to use which I think must be very specifically war time or pre-war time and it means are you kidding*

OED (1781) 'slang'

ANTWACK adj. old-fashioned

Liverpool (male, 1959, C1442/02638) *the word is antwack and it means old-fashioned and I think it may well come from a phonetic spelling of antique*

NPD (2002) *antwacky* 'UK (Liverpool)'

APPLES AND PEARS n. stairs

London (female, C1442/03160) *I'm a Londoner born and bred my father especially had a very Cockney accent and we often at home referred to up the apples and pears when we had to go up to bed*

London (male, 1949, C1442/00214) *Cockney slang apples and pears stairs*

Stepney (female, 1940, C1442/01213) *up the apples and pears from the era of the Pearly Kings and Queens when people were rushing around and rushing up ladders and going up stairs and rushing to catch buses and trains*

OED (1857) 'rhyming slang'

ATTIC n. garret, room in loft

Huddersfield (female, 1944, C1442/01952) *I've noticed that people call their bedrooms up in the roof space a loft these days but we always still call it an attic and sometimes people from the south wonder why I refer to it as the attic when there's a bedroom in it*

OED (1817)

B

BACK-JIGGER n. alleyway

Liverpool (male, 1934, C1442/00156) *back-jigger is an alleyway which runs between two blocks of houses where the bin men can come and take the rubbish and it has access to the rear of the houses*

OED (1902) 'Merseyside'

cf. GENNEL, GINNEL, JITTY, SNICKET, TWITCHEL, TWITTEN

IStock Photo

BAFFIE n. slipper

Fife (female, 1958, C1442/00849) *I like the word baffies which in my family from the east coast of Scotland has always been used for slippers I've always loved the sound of it it's got a kind of cosy warm feel just because of the type of footwear it's for so I think it's a really appropriate word and I like using it*

IStock Photo

DSL (1914) *baff* poss. derived from *bauchle* (1787) [= 'old shoe, loose slipper']

BAGGING n. snack, packed lunch

Lancashire (female, 168, C1442/02126) *bagging means a snack I assume it comes from the bag they put the snack in I don't know but it's commonly used amongst the farmers in the west of Lancashire*

OED (1746) 'dialect'

cf. DOCKEY

BANJO vb. to beat, thrash, hit

Newcastle upon Tyne (female, 1931, C1442/01660) *people say when you are angry you'll banjo them I don't know where that comes from*

DSL (1975)

cf. BRAY, DECK

BANTEROUS adj. playful, jocular, full of banter

Poole (female, 1993, C1442/02202) *banterous is joking and messing around with friends and private jokes that you have with each other*

DCS (2013)

NOTES In April 2013 a Daily Telegraph article by Lizzie Porter examined organised student drinking bouts from a feminist perspective prompted by a sense of unease at the link between drunkenness and promiscuity. What emerged as an equally interesting theme was the importance some women attached to keeping up with so-called male 'banter'. Porter used a couple of interesting neologisms, commenting that some women set great store by being able to 'out-banter' their male peers, while also referencing a 'banterous' online review. Having three teenage children I can certainly vouch for the fact that banter is a default setting for much communication in our family and, more importantly, between our children and their friends, and I have enjoyed observing similar linguistic innovation. Periods of sustained banter are dubbed 'bantathons' or trips to 'Bantasy Island' and individuals admired for particularly impressive banter I have heard anointed 'the Archbishop of Banterbury', 'Eric Bantona', 'Banta Claus', 'Bantosaurus Rex' or 'Captain Bantastic'.

cf. SNEET

BARE adj. lots of; adv. very

London (male, 1991, C1442/02447) *bare means a lot I was very confused when I first heard it in about 2003 I don't know how it came about at all B A R E is how most people spell it somehow people have a collective knowledge of how it's spelt which is pretty weird so you would use the word like 'I've just got paid I've got bare money now' you know 'it's bare cold' very very cold that type of thing*

London (male, 1992, C1442/00666) *when something's bare funny you go 'LMAO' and it means laughing my arse off so if someone says something funny you go 'LMAO' it's bare jokes*

GDS (2003)

BARMPOT n. fool (used affectionately)

Glasgow (male, 1950, C1442/01118) *barmpot is used in Glasgow it describes someone who's more than just silly or crazy but it's not done in a malicious way it's done in a friendly way 'he was a complete barmpot' it could've been someone who told jokes or when someone was drunk they were dancing about crazily and people in England or anywhere else are always intrigued because I've never heard it anywhere else other than Glasgow*

Willenhall (female, 1954, C1442/00529) *my dad used to say somebody was a bit of a barmpot being a bit silly*

OED (1951) 'English regional'

cf. BARMPOT, BUMBLEKLUTZ, DAFT/SOPPY HA'PORTH, EEJIT, GIMP, NUMPTY, PLANK, WAZZOCK, TWONK, WUMPERT

BEAUT n. a beauty, stunner

Barnet (female, 1993, C1442/01094) *beaut it means attractive and I would use it when I see a hot guy I would say 'he's a beaut'*

OED (1866) 'slang (originally Australian and New Zealand)'

cf. BOOM–TING, BUFF TING

BEETHY adj. soft, over–ripe

Wolverhampton (male, 1947, C1442/00311) *my father came from Shropshire and if an apple was soft and pappy and not very pleasant to eat he'd call that beethy*

EDD (1790)

cf. DWINGEY, FOZY, MAUMY

IStock Photo

BISHY-BARNABEE n. ladybird

London (female, 1953, C1442/01306) *I live now in Norfolk and a lovely word is bishy-barnabee which is the local word for a ladybird and it comes I believe from Bishop Barnaby in Middle Ages who used to wear a red cloak*

EDD (1855) *Bishop Barnabee* East Anglia

IStock Photo

BITS AND BATS n. bits and pieces, bits and bobs

Leeds (male, 1561, C1442/01566) *bits and bats means bits and pieces*

OED (1896)

cf. TRANKLEMENTS

BLACK OVER BILL'S MOTHER'S phr. expression used of imminent rain

Nottingham (male, 1991, C1442/00951) *it's a bit black over Bill's mother's I think it's from Long Eaton maybe Nottinghamshire Derbyshire border and you say it when the sky's a bit dark or grey and it basically means it's gonna rain*

Dictionary of Catch Phrases British and American (1985); VOICES confirms use in East Midlands and *black over Will's mother's* in Kent

cf. ENOUGH BLUE SKY TO MAKE A SAILOR A PAIR OF TROUSERS

BLART vb. to bleat, cry, whimper

Wolverhampton (female, 1977, C1442/00383) *I like blarting for crying 'oh she was blarting and blarting' I think it's a really expressive word*

OED (1896) 'dialect'

cf. SKRIKE

BOBBINS adj. rubbish, useless

UK (female, 1973, C1442/00700) *bobbins I first encountered at university fifteen years ago when there was somebody from Grimsby who I liked a lot and therefore picked up some of his words and in our shared house it was one of our shared words and bobbins means a bit rubbish in a deliberately slightly childish deprecating way*

South (male, 1959, C1442/01066) *I'm really a southerner living in Manchester but a friend of mine used to use bobbins if something was not good rubbish as other people might say he'd say 'oh that's bobbins' I've no idea where that came from maybe from the mills but I quite enjoy that phrase*

GDS (1998)

cf. GASH, JARG

NOTES I associate *bobbins* most readily with Manchester and particularly enjoyed hearing it used by professional Mancunian Liam Gallagher when he appeared as a guest on Channel 4's *The F Word* in 2008. Asked by presenter Gordon Ramsey to comment on the food, he said he had enjoyed it but added *your sweet potato was bobbins man my missus does better than that.*

BOBBY-DAZZLER n. someone/something striking or excellent

Lancashire (male, 1939, C1442/00189) *I use bobby-dazzler it means somebody who's very good at something*

OED (1866) 'originally and chiefly dialect'

BOB-OWLER n. large moth

Birmingham (male, 1954, C1442/01637) *bob-owler which my father used he was from Birmingham meaning something like a moth some little flying insect that would be fluttering behind the curtains*

EDD (1878); VOICES Dudley (C1190/05/02) *blotto as a bob-owler* [= 'drunk']

BOKE vb. to retch, gasp for air prior to vomiting

Stirling (female, 1998, C1442/00105) *to say that's something's disgusting or makes you feel sick you'd say 'it's gieing me the boke' and it means that you're disgusted by it basically*

EDD North & East Midlands

cf. CHUNDER, GIP, HUGHIE

BONKOID adj. odd, weird

South East (female, C1442/02280) *bonkoid I use with a couple of people it was a neologism but I've actually seen it on Google as well I searched the word bonkoid and there are quite a few hits we made it up because things that are wonky we started calling wonkoid a bit like something being cuboid and we extended that to bonkoid to mean something that is bonkers or a bit weird in some way*

GDS (1900) –*oid* [= productive suffix used 'to express a brainless or automatic quality']; DCS –*oid* [= 'negative version of neutral –*ish* or –*esque*']

BOOM-TING n. attractive person

Oxford (female, 1993, C1442/00952) *we say the word boom-ting or buff ting which started off as a joke because people that we didn't really like used it and then we started using it more and more and now we use it in everyday language*

DCS (1990s)

cf. cf. BEAUT, BUFF (TING), HOT, PENG, TICK

BOSS adj. great, excellent

Widnes (female, 1989, C1442/00488) *boss it means good great I think it comes from Liverpool and it's used by almost all people*

NPD (1873)

cf. CANNY, CHAMPION, CUSHTY, GRAND, LUSH, MINT, NANG, SICK, WICK

BOSS-EYED adj. cross-eyed

Barnet (female, C1442/02420) *boss-eyed means cross-eyed somebody who doesn't see straight ahead I live in Merseyside and I find nobody in that area will understand that word*

OED (1860) 'dialect and slang'

IStock Photo

NOTES This is a word I am particularly fond of, as my wife was the first person I ever heard say it, although unlike this speaker she always pronounces it 'bozz-eyed'. SED fieldwork recorded several regional variants for 'cross-eyed' including *glee-eyed* in the North East, *skend* in Lancashire, *squint-eyed* in East Anglia and the West Country and *boss-eyed* in the Midlands and South. Intriguingly, although 'boss-eyed' was recorded frequently across the southern half of England there are only two instances where informants supplied a pronunciation with a medial <-z-> sound – one in a village in Derbyshire and the other in Staffordshire. My wife grew up near Ashbourne on the Staffordshire–Derbyshire border and was understandably intrigued to discover her pronunciation is such a localised form and that her 20-year old nephew also pronounces it that way.

BRAY vb. to beat, thrash, hit

North Yorkshire (female, 1987, C1442/02704) *my favourite two words from my home town are deck and bray which mean attack someone*

OED (1808) 'dialect'

cf. BANJO, DECK

BUBBE n. grandmother

Hackney (female, 1949, C1442/02383) *like my mother and grandmother I'm called bubbe it means grandma and comes from Yiddish my grandchildren call me bubbe quite often you're called by your first name as well so I am bubbe Michelle my children called my mother bubbe and as a result all my friends call my mother bubbe because she prefers that to her first name*

OED (1895) 'Yiddish'

cf. ZAYDE

BUBBLE, HAVE A vb. to have a laugh, joke

East London (female, 1992, C1442/00535) *we use some rhyming slang still not an awful lot but like having a bubble you're having a laugh having a bubble bath*

London (male, C1442/02263) *you're having a bubble mate I think that came from the East End of London when they spoke Cockney some years ago*

DCS 'contemporary synonym for archaic version *tin bath*'

NOTES Although no longer restricted to Cockneys, rhyming slang is so closely associated with speech in the capital that representations of London dialect invariably include examples. In an episode of BBC soap opera *EastEnders* in May 2014 Nick Carter, the latest in a long line of landlords of the Queen Vic pub, presented his daughter, Nancy, with a pair of boxing gloves saying *I borrowed them from the gym now don't hold back whack these on, girl*. Somewhat taken aback, Nancy's response was *you having a bubble?* Although by no means a regular viewer I subsequently kept an ear out for other examples and in the month of May 2014 alone Tina Carter exited the Queen Vic pub with the line *tell Mick I ain't got a scooby* [i.e. Scooby-Doo = 'clue'] *when we're gonna get back in the flat* and the recently returned Dean Wicks told Linda Carter *I could definitely do something with that barnet* [i.e. Barnet Fair = 'hair'].

BUFF adj. physically attractive

Stepney (male, 1975, C1442/01581) *attractive I would say buff 'oh that's buff, mate, she's buff'*

East London (female, 1993, C1442/00535) *for attractive we'll say buff it's supposed to mean someone who's well-built and quite muscly but it kind of ends up meaning someone who's attractive*

London (female, C1442/00398) *some people in London use for attractive buff*

OED (1982) 'slang (originally US)'

cf. BOOM-TING, BUFF TING, HOT, PENG, TICK

BUFFET n. footstool

Yorkshire (male, 1956, C1442/00098) *buffet we always used in our family to mean what other people usually call a stool*

OED (1432) 'now only Scottish and northern dialect'

BUFF TING n. attractive person

South East (male, 1995, C1442/01069) *buff ting we use for attractive and it comes from slang*

South East (female, 1997, C1442/00394) *buff ting is like attractive*

London (male, 1988, C1442/02265) *buff ting I dunno where that comes from I think it's a slang term but it can define an extremely beautiful person*

London (female, C1442/00465) *attractive I probably never say this but a lot of people say 'he's a buff ting'*

Oxford (female, 1993, C1442/00952) *we say the word boom-ting or buff ting which started off as a joke because people that we didn't really like used it and then we started using it more and more and now we use it in everyday language*

UD (2002)

cf. cf. BEAUT, BOOM-TING, BUFF, HOT, PENG, TICK

BUMBLEKLUTZ n. fool (used affectionately)

Ealing (male, C1442/01253) *bumbleklutz is applied in my family to someone who isn't quite competent particularly when playing a game or playing cards who doesn't follow suit or does something a bit silly*

GDS (1956) *bumbo-claat* 'West Indian term of abuse'; UD (2011) *bumbleklut*

cf. BARMPOT, BUMBOCLOT, DAFT/SOPPY HA'PORTH, EEJIT, GIMP, NUMPTY, PLANK, WAZZOCK, TWONK, WUMPERT

BUMBOCLOT n. fool (used affectionately)

Liverpool (male, C1442/00177) *bumboclot means idiot*

GDS (1956) *bumbo-claat* 'West Indian term of abuse'

cf. BARMPOT, BUMBLEKLUTZ, DAFT/SOPPY HA'PORTH, EEJIT, GIMP, NUMPTY, PLANK, WAZZOCK, TWONK, WUMPERT

BUNCE n. money

London (male, 1981, C1442/00459) *bunce is money if you're bunced up you have a lot of money got no bunce no money I don't know where it comes from my girlfriend uses it a lot she's from Sheffield and her and a number of her friends use it a lot*

OED (1706) 'slang'

IStock Photo

cf. MOOLAH

BUSSLE vb. to bother, pester, annoy

London (female, 1999, C1442/01780) *bussle that's a word I made up it means when someone is annoying you and keeps on hassling you I made it up when I was little and now I use it a lot* [C1442/02435]

cf. CHAUVE, MITHER, MOITHER

BUTTERS adj. physically unattractive, ugly

London (female, 1981, C1442/00646) *for unattractive there's butters*

London (female, 1993, C1442/01248) *butters means ugly and I don't know where it comes from at all*

London (female) *some people in London use for ugly butters* [C1442/00398]

London (female, C1442/00535) *for unattractive butters I don't know where that comes from I think most of the slang in East London ends up being Caribbean I don't know whether it is but I've always thought it is but I've no idea*

London Nigerian (female, 1996) *butters means that you're really ugly it's basically a minger but butters is worse* [C1442/00410]

East London (female, 1993) *for unattractive butters* [C1442/00535]

Harrogate (female, 1985) *unattractive is butters I guess it means if someone's got a butter-face and it's all melted and mashed up I guess* [C1442/00410]

NPD (2002) 'UK slang'; NPD (2003) *butter-face* [= 'girl or woman with attractive body and unprepossessing face']

cf. GOPPING, HOWFING, MINGING

C

CANNY adj. great, excellent; adv. very, really, fairly

County Durham (female, 1981, C1442/00967) *one word which we use all the time is canny it's a completely superfluous word and we use it to emphasise adjectives so you would say that something was canny massive or canny small or it can also mean that someone's nice if you say they are canny*

Middlesbrough (female, 1977, C1442/02660) *I like the use of the word canny in the North East canny means clever or wily when it's used in the south whereas in the north it describes a quality that I can't think of another word which could be used in its place you'd say somebody's a canny lad and it's a compliment and a reflection of the fact that they're not so much cute but endearing it often suggests a certain kindness but also attractiveness a canny lad or a canny lass is usually used for something endearing in young people*

OED (1637) 'north of England and Scotland (with different senses)'

cf. BOSS, CHAMPION, CUSHTY, GRAND, LUSH, MINT, NANG, SICK, WICK

CARNAPTIOUS adj. bad-tempered, moody, quarrelsome

Northern Ireland (male, 1956, C1442/00850) *carnaptious means awkward difficult such as 'he's in a very carnaptious mood'*

OED (1858) 'Scottish and Irish dialect'

cf. MARDY, MAUNGY

CASSENED adj. flat on one's back, unable to stand up, i.e. 'exhausted, tired out'

Cumbria (female, C1442/00514) *my mother's favourite expression when she was very very tired was I's cassened and it meant I'm really tired in farm speak if you see a sheep on its back unable to get back on its feet without help cassened was the term that was used*

EDD & SED *cassened* [= 'overturned (of sheep)']

cf. FANNAKAPANNED, JIGGERED, WABBIT

CHAMPION adj. great, excellent

South (female, 1935, C1442/00893) *champion it's a Tyneside word and it means just fine*

OED (1914) 'colloquial or dialect'

cf. BOSS, CANNY, CUSHTY, LUSH, MINT, NANG, SICK, WICK

CHARNOCK phr. mad, insane (i.e. reference to local psychiatric hospital)

St Helens (female, 1955, C1442/01328) *the phrase my grandmother used which always made us all smile she'd talk about somebody having had her time at Charnock which I understood as a child was a Lancashire place name and I think there was some kind of psychiatric hospital there because the general understanding was that somebody had been there and were coming back out into society again it was one of those phrases that was always muttered with a sort of knowingness that was slightly bewildering as a child but granny would always say 'she'd had her time at Charnock' and we were supposed to know what it meant*

NOTES. I am sure many of us would admit with embarrassment that we either used or were aware of this sort of reference in the past. Greater sensitivity to mental illness and learning difficulties and the closure of some of the more austere establishments has meant that such terms are, I suspect, increasingly rare nowadays. I cringe now but as a teenager in Sutton Coldfield I recall odd behaviour or moments of stupidity were often greeted with the comment *are you from Langley* (i.e. the local special school). Evidence from VOICES suggests this was a widespread phenomenon as confirmed by analogous phrases apparently used in the past including *Barnsley Hall bloke* (Dudley, C1190/05/02); *if you aren't careful they'll send you to Hellesdon* (Horsford, C1190/24/03); *you should be in De La Pole with the nut jobs* (Hull, C1190/16/04); *you'll end up in Millbrook* (Kirkby-in-Ashfield, C1190/26/03); *escaped from Meadowbrook* (Salford, C1190/04/05); and *fit for Bodmin* (Bodmin, C1190/10/01).

CHAUVE vb. to annoy

Wigan (female, 1989, C1442/01011) *if you were chauving someone you would actually be annoying them so someone would say 'stop chauving me' or 'he's chauving me'*

EDD (1839) North

cf. BUSSLE, MITHER, MOITHER

CHAUVE vb. to get by, struggle along

Aberdeen (female, 1987, C1442/01984) *when I call to see my mum if I ask her how she's doing she says 'oh just chauving awa' which means just managing just carrying on as normal I think that's a really cute phrase*

DSL (1637) Banffshire and Aberdeenshire

CHIRPS vb. to flirt with, set one's cap at someone

South East (male, 1994, C1442/00081) *chirps means that you like someone if Chris was chirpsing Louise he would be looking to go out with her*

NPD (2004)

CHOBBLE vb. to gobble, chew, eat noisily

Wolverhampton (female, 1977, C1442/00383) *growing up in Wolverhampton lots of the friends I hung around with had great words like to chobble a sweet 'she's chobbling it' it's a boiled sweet and it's making that noise in your mouth as you suck it*

EDD West Midlands

CHUBBLE vb. to guess contents of parcel prior to opening

UK (male, 1958, C1442/02707) *chubble is a word for finding out what's in a parcel usually a Christmas parcel by picking it up feeling it shaking it listening to it to work out what the present is before you open it it's something that is used usually when we're sitting around and it's 'don't chubble because you'll guess what the present is' to the extent we even buy presents for each other to make it almost impossible to chubble them*

CHUNDER vb. to vomit

Reading (female, 1995, C1442/00955) *chunder means be sick and throw up but it's quite humorous because there was this video on YouTube that went global about some person and the gap year and it was really funny and it's evolved and become part of everyday speech it's usually used in connotations of drinking too much so you'd go out and then you'd chunder because you were drunk rather than necessarily because you were ill but it's quite a jokes word*

OED (1950) 'Australian slang'

cf. BOKE, GIP, HUGHIE

CLARTY adj. sticky, gooey

North (female, C1442/00026) *clarty is a slang word for messy sticky just a northern saying*

Nottingham (female, 1937, C1442/01880) *clarty sticky a clarty pudding is something that would stick to the roof of your mouth*

OED (1855) 'northern dialect'

NOTES This word occurs in several dialects in a variety of forms with different senses. In the North East of England the noun *clarts* has traditionally been used of 'sticky mud'. An SED informant recorded in Lowick, Northumberland in the 1950s reported an important local distinction between *clarts* [= 'thick, sticky mud'] and *glaur* [= 'thin, wet mud'] and a speaker from Newcastle upon Tyne, recorded for a British Library oral history project in 1998 (C900/11129), recalled his days as a young labourer when he would happily jump off the back of the lorry and head straight into the pub *all covered in clarts*. This is confirmed by a WordBank contributor from Sunderland (C1442/01617) who recalls enjoying *plodging in the clarts* [= 'paddling in mud'] as a child. By extension, *clarts* is also commonly used in the North East for 'excrement' – particularly in the phrase *in the clarts* [= 'in the shit', i.e. 'in deep trouble'] – as confirmed by an entry in NPD (1977). A

VOICES recording in Telford (C1190/29/02) also captures a speaker using the closely related adjective *clatty* in the sense of 'dirty, tarty, sexually promiscuous'.

CLEMMED adj. hungry, starving

Wigan (male, 1949, C1442/01091) *I have a word from when I was a small child for hungry clemmed I understand it's originally Scandinavian but it's widely used in my part of Lancashire*

OED (1674) 'dialect'

CLIT n. knot, tangle (in hair)

London (female, 1951, C1442/02529) *clit is a word that my mum from the Isle of Wight used to use for the knots in my hair when she was combing it it's not a word I've ever heard anywhere else so I assume it was from the Isle of Wight*

IStock Photo

EDD Hampshire

cf. LUG

COB n. bread roll

Nottingham (female, 1937, C1442/01880) *cob a small bread roll normally quite a crisp one*

OED (1609) 'dialect'

cf. ROWIE, STOTTY

IStock Photo

COB ON, HAVE A vb. to be in a bad mood, act moodily

Doncaster (male, 1949, C1442/00559) *if a younger child is not happy down south near Nottingham you'd say it'd got a cob on*

GDS (1982)

cf. PADDY

COIN vb. to corner, turn a corner

Newcastle upon Tyne (male, 1928, C1442/00997) *so I bowled doun the road coined the corner and dunched into the wall*

EDD *coin* [= noun 'corner'] North East

COLLY NOB n. Brussels sprout

Derby (male, 1965, C1442/01641) *colly nob means a Brussels sprout and is a corruption of kaley nob*

Ey Up Mi Duck! (Richard Scollins & John Titford, 1976); VOICES Groby (C1190/20/03) *nob*

COOPER'S DUCKS phr. the end is nigh

Dudley (male, 1989, C1442/01477) *a phrase to describe the end death things like that would be it's Cooper's Ducks this is a phrase engraved on a gravestone in a cemetery not too far away it's got to be some reference to a local character called Cooper who had ducks that may have died in a sudden unfortunate incident but Cooper's Ducks is a very interesting way of saying the end is nigh*

Shropshire Words and Dialect (Valerie Kilford, 1981) *Cooper's Ducks* [= 'that's the end/that's your lot']

CRAIC n. fun, amusement

Dublin (male, 1988, C1442/02316) *craic means having fun and you would say 'having the craic' 'I had the craic last night' 'we all had the craic' 'it was good craic'*

OED (1972) 'Irish'

CROGGIE n. shared ride on handlebars of bicycle

Kimberley, Nottinghamshire (male, 1986, C1442/01748) *a croggie is when two people are riding a bike one person sitting on the saddle one person in front of them I think that's something to do with the crossbar*

DCS (2003) 'schoolchildren's slang'

NOTES Anecdotal evidence suggests this is a relatively widely used abbreviation of 'crossbar' formed by analogy with a number of words used particularly by young speakers such as *plaggy* or *placky* [= 'plastic'] and *laggy* or *lacky* [= 'elastic']. The underlying form often contains a medial <-st-> sound which mutates to <g> or <k> and the final syllable is replaced by the suffix <-y>. I certainly have very fond memories of winters in the 1970s and hoping for enough snow to go *plackybagging* [= 'sledging on a plastic bag/bin liner'] and always keeping a *lacky band* [= 'elastic band'] in my school blazer pocket to fire paper pellets with. I even heard a university friend from Newcastle apply this process to create the term *fantackerbacker* [= 'fantastic']. NPD (2006) confirms *plaggy* [= 'plastic'] and UD (2008)

IStock Photo

records *lacky band* for 'elastic band', while *The Lore of the Playground* (Steve Roud, 2010) includes *laggies* as one of several regional variants for a skipping game played with a long elastic band (aka French skipping).

CUSHTY adj. great, excellent

Newcastle upon Tyne (female, 1994, C1442/01680) *cushty means class*

South (male, 1995, C1442/02667) *cushty meaning sort of very good cool or something like that I'd use it with friends*

OED (1929) 'British slang'

cf. BOSS, CANNY, CHAMPION, GRAND, LUSH, MINT, NANG, SICK, WICK

CWTCH n. cuddle, snuggle

South Wales (female, 1987, C1442/02236) *where I'm from it's very common to say cwtch which means having a cuddle or getting physically close maybe on a sofa to your friend or maybe your mum and dad or your boyfriend or girlfriend it encompasses a prolonged action rather than just one cuddle you have a cwtch and it lasts a long time it's used by my family my parents my little sister and a lot of my friends have appropriated it as well*

OED (1992) 'Welsh English'

D

DAFT HA'PORTH n. fool (used affectionately)

Blackburn (female, 1985, C1442/00290) *I use you daft ha'porth I think it's from you silly halfpenny piece and I would use it with my friends if I thought they were being a bit silly I'd say 'oh you daft ha'porth'*

GDS (1950) *soft ha'porth*; GDS (1977) *soppy ha'porth*

cf. BARMPOT, BUMBLEKLUTZ, BUMBOCLOT, EEJIT, GIMP, NUMPTY, PLANK, SOPPY HA'PORTH, TWONK, WAZZOCK, WUMPERT

DAP n. plimsoll, child's soft shoe worn for PE

Somerset (female, 1960, C1442/01598) *in our house we call plimsolls daps which comes from Somerset but the rest of the family who come from the North East of England always refer to them as sand-shoes*

Wiltshire (female, 1950, C1442/00751) *a word we used in Wiltshire was daps for plimsolls something you'd get changed into when children did PE as a teacher I would always use 'go and put your daps on' and children in other parts of the country didn't understand that and I had to explain it*

OED (1924) 'colloquial and dialect'

cf. SAND-SHOE

DEAF vb. to forego an activity/event, to pack something/someone in

Birmingham (male, 1975, C1442/00379) *a verb we used as children at school as in to deaf somebody so if you were a couple and you were going out if you were to deaf them that means you'd be splitting up and no longer be going out I've never heard it outside of the Midlands*

NOTES Research suggests many speakers use dialect forms more frequently in their formative years and in later life than during their middle years, probably due to the dense social networks we typically maintain at either end of our lives compared with the more fluid nature of our working lives. Five words I distinctly remember using regularly as a child and teenager in Sutton Coldfield in the 1970s but which subsequently drifted from my active repertoire were *barley* [= truce term used in game of *tig*], *bosting* [= 'great, excellent'], *crash* [= 'to share'], *class* [= 'to complete, finish', esp. in reference to collections of e.g.

stamps, football stickers or World Cup coins] and, like this speaker, *deaf*.

An impressive range of truce terms is still heard in playgrounds, parks and streets across the country as confirmed by WordBank entries for *fainites, skinchies, squadsies, squitsies* and *thousies. The Lore and Language of Schoolchildren* (Peter & Iona Opie, 1959) confirms *barley* is used in a large area of the UK extending from the West Midlands and North West of England and along the East Coast of Scotland. Curiously DCS records *bosting* as an East Midlands and North West dialect form, although I sense it is restricted to the West Midlands – an impression corroborated by all the entries in the OED and at UD. Indeed its status as an iconic Brummy and Black Country term of approval is confirmed by the website bostin.org.uk, which advertises a range of T-shirts featuring local dialect phrases and claims the Black Country Bible opens with the line *In the Beginning there was the Word. And the word was Bostin.* I also associate *bosting* with that legendary fictional West Midlander, Barry Taylor, the Wolverhampton electrician played by Timothy Spall in 1980s comedy-drama *Auf Wiedersehen, Pet.*

The word *crash* I remember shouting if ever anyone produced a bag of sweets or crisps in the hope of persuading them to share their snack. Reassuringly NPD (1977) records *crash* as teenage slang for 'to give something out' and includes a citation in nearby Leicestershire. For *class* I have yet to find any corroborating evidence, although I remember using it frequently, particularly in conversations about football stickers as in *have you got Ian Wallace yet … yeah so I only need Barry Powell now and I've classed Cov* (i.e. 'completed the full set of Coventry City stickers'). A typical example of how we used *deaf* would be *are you going to the pictures tonight … no I haven't got any money I'm gonna deaf it;* and until I stumbled – with great excitement – across this speaker I had not heard the term since I was a teenager. Frustratingly I am yet to find any record in other sources, although I can confirm young speakers nowadays have a variety of analogous phrases such as *bun it, sack that* or *allow.* Perhaps then, *deaf* might have been the slang expression of its day, although as the two uses I am aware of are from Birmingham it seems reasonable to suggest it was (maybe still is) a localised form.

DECK vb. to beat, thrash, hit

North Yorkshire (female, 1987, C1442/02704) *my favourite two words from my home town are deck and bray which mean attack someone*

OED (1953) 'slang (originally US)'

cf. BANJO, BRAY

DERBY (ROAD) adj. cold

Nottingham (male, 1966, C1442/01310) *in Nottingham if it's cold we say 'it's a bit Derby' it's kind of rhyming slang we have a famous road called Derby Road but a lot of people in Nottingham seem to drop the L when they say cold so they say cowd so it rhymes with Derby Road so if someone says 'ooh it's Derby' they mean it's cold*

Nottingham (male, 1969, C1442/00684) *in Nottingham we might say it's cowd instead of it's cold and if we're feeling frisky we might actually turn that into rhyming slang so it's a bit Derby Road obviously rhyming with cowd meaning cold and we particularly don't like Derby in Nottingham so it's doubly funny*

UD (2008) 'Nottingham rhyming slang'

cf. NITHERED, PARKY, TATERS, THANDA

NOTES Rhyming slang is a wonderful vehicle for individual and collective linguistic creativity. This expression also captures playful rivalry between neighbouring cities so you can sense the enjoyment with which it might be used in Nottingham. The Derby Road merges into a long stretch of the A52 recently re-named 'Brian Clough Way' in honour of the football manager who enjoyed unprecedented success at both Derby County and Nottingham Forest. Despite the fierce rivalry between the two clubs, he is viewed with equal affection in both cities, so this simple phrase conveys much more to a local than outsiders can possibly imagine.

DIMPSY adj. twilight, dusk

Newton Abbot (male, 1975, C1442/00795) *getting dark when I look into the dusky sky I say it's getting dimpsy*

Somerset (female, 1963, C1442/02734) *dimpsy that's twilight*

OED (1693) *dimps* 'dialect'

IStock Photo

DING vb. to microwave

Wiltshire (female, 1989, C1442/00702) *to microwave something is to ding it as in 'would you go and ding this chocolate muffin for me'*

GDS (1995) *ding* [= 'telephone'] 'West Indies' but no record in this sense

DOCKEY n. snack, packed lunch

The Fens (male, 1943, C1442/02306) *dockey means what you would eat out in the fields if you were a farmer and you'd take maybe an apple and some cheese with you you'd call it your dockey I don't know the origin of the word but I think it might have something to do with the farm hands could be docked pay for the time they spent eating I've heard that explanation but I think it's speculative but it's a word that I've only ever heard in East Anglia particularly in the Fen country*

EDD (1819)

cf. BAGGING

DODMAN n. snail

Norfolk (female, 1953, C1442/02091) *a dodman is Norfolk for a snail*

OED (1625) 'now dialect'

DOG AND BONE n. telephone

London (male, 1949, C1442/00214) *dog and bone phone*

OED (1961) 'rhyming slang'

IStock Photo

DONKER n. TV remote control

London (female, 1948, C1442/01191) *donker for the remote control it just came up rather than saying remote control*

KTL (2008)

cf. DOOFER

DOOFER n. TV remote control

Wiltshire (female, 1989, C1442/00702) *in my family we use doofer to mean television remote as in have you seen the doofer I guess 'cause it means the thingy*

OED (1937) *doofer* [= 'thingummy']; NPD (1945) *doofer* [= 'gadget']; KTL (2008) *doofer* [= 'TV remote control']

cf. DONKER

IStock Photo

DRECKLY adv. presently, in a while

Cornwall (female, 1986, C1442/01827) *Cornishmen do things dreckly*

Cornwall (female, C1442/01470) *Cornish word for later some time mañana*

EDD South West, West Country and rural South East

DREICH adj. dreary, dull, gloomy

Glasgow (female, 1956, C1442/01297) *one used regularly is dreich for some reason in the phrase 'it's gey dreich' means it's very grey and grim*

DSL (1856) 'General Scots, also in northern English dialect'

DUNCH vb. to butt, bump, knock

Tyneside (male, 1928, C1442/00209) *the word dunch is a collision 'divven't dunch us' is don't collide into us*

Newcastle upon Tyne (male, 1928, C1442/00997) *so I bowled doun the road coined the corner and dunched into the wall*

OED (1240) 'chiefly dialect'

DWILE n. floor cloth, flannel

Norfolk (male, 1947, C1442/02003) *dwile a heavy-duty cleaning cloth*

OED (1823) 'dialect'

DWINGEY adj. spongy, shrivelled, over-ripe

Norfolk (male, 1947, C1442/02003) *dwingey shrivelled or shrunken like a tomato or grape or flower*

OED (c.1000) *dwine* [= 'to wither']; EDD *dwinge* [= 'to shrivel']

cf. BEETHY, FOZY, MAUMY

E

EEJIT n. fool (used affectionately)

Dublin (female, 1958, C1442/00608) *I like the word eejit which we use extensively where I come from it means idiot but not really as rude as idiot it's more a friendly sort of an eejit and can be said quite affectionately or a little bit more aggressively when somebody's done something really dumb*

NPD (1955) 'Irish'

cf. BARMPOT, BUMBLEKLUTZ, BUMBOCLOT, DAFT/SOPPY HA'PORTH, GIMP, NUMPTY, PLANK, TWONK, WAZZOCK, WUMPERT

EMMET n. ant, (and, by extension) tourist

Yeovil (female, 1964, C1442/02760) *emmets is ants there's lots of West Country dialect that we have for local animals and plants that people really wouldn't know emmets happens to be a bit like grockles for tourists if you call them emmets or grockles it means you're not very happy with them and you wish they'd all go back home and leave you in peace it's like they're ants coming all over everything so that's why I like them words* [C1442/02760]

OED (c.1300) *emmet* [= 'ant'] 'regional'; OED (1975) *emmet* [= 'tourist'] 'humorous'; NPD (1978) confirms present-day use in sense of 'tourist'

cf. GROCKLE

ENOUGH BLUE SKY TO MAKE A SAILOR A PAIR OF TROUSERS phr. expression used on seeing two patches of blue sky on stormy day (i.e. implying improvement in weather)

Grimsby (female, 1939, C1442/01378) *I often use the expression there's enough blue sky to make a sailor's pair of trousers and none of my friends seem to have heard of it so I don't know if it's a peculiarity to my family or if it does actually exist*

Brewer's Dictionary of Phrase & Fable 19th Edition (ed. Susie Dent, 2012) *enough blue sky to make a Dutchman a pair of breeches* 'nautical'; *Phrases & Sayings* (Nigel Rees, 1995) *enough blue sky to make a sailor a pair of trousers*

cf. BLACK OVER BILL'S MOTHERS

F

FAINITES excl. truce term guaranteeing immunity from capture in children's game

London (male, 1934, C1442/01873) *when I was a boy we used to say fainites and cross our fingers to stop whatever it was we were doing chasing each other this is a different expression from my wife's in Nuneaton I can't remember what hers is but it's totally different she'd never heard of mine before*

OED (1870) 'school slang, originally dialect'; *The Lore and Language of Schoolchildren* (Peter & Iona Opie, 1959) *fainites* London and South East

cf. SKINCHIES, SQUADSIES, SQUITSIES, THOUSIES

FANKLE vb. to tangle, entangle

Glasgow (female, 1956, C1442/01297) *fankle which we use for when things are in a knot*

OED (1724) 'Scottish'

FANNAKAPANNED adj. exhausted, tired out

Fife (female, 1957, C1442/00020) *fannakapanned is a word I use to describe myself when I'm feeling tired or exhausted* cf. CASSENED, JIGGERED, WABBIT

NOTES Although I have not found any record of *fannakapan* in this sense there are several online references – notably in Lancashire and Lincolnshire – to *Fred* (or *Fanny*) *Fannakapan* being used affectionately to and of children who are doing something endearingly silly. 'Fred Fannakapan' is the title of a 1938 popular song written by Reginald Low for Gracie Fields so perhaps it is just one of those funny-sounding names that catch people's imagination from time to time and are adopted to serve a variety of purposes – my dad has been known to use *Fred Ippititimouse* (presumably influenced by the comedy character, Alf Ippititimus, created and played by actor Jack Douglas) in much the same way to refer to anyone acting foolishly.

FANTABULOUS adj. ridiculous, outrageous, absurd

Newcastle (female, 1990, C1442/01671) *the word is fantabulous it comes from two words fantastic and fabulous and basically it's made up by my friends and myself but I think a lot of other people use it as well it's just a very good exclamation word*

GDS (1953)

cf. RIDONKULOUS

FEMMER adj. fragile, weak, easily broken

Darlington (male, 1970, C1442/01772) *a Durham coal miner's word if somebody is femmer they're weak*

EDD (1870)

cf. FUSHIONLESS, PEELY-WALLY, SHILPIT

FIPER vb. to show affected modesty

Cambridge (female, 1948, C1442/02709) *in our family we have a rather wicked habit of turning the names of close relatives or friends into verbs fipering is from a friend of ours Mr Fipers who was always rather falsely modest about things as children if we were being falsely modest we were told to stop fipering*

FOOTER vb. to potter about, while away time

Ballymena (female, 1949, C1442/01189) *if somebody says to me 'what did you do today' I say 'och I was just footering about' I believe it might be from Scottish dialect 'cause I'm from Northern Ireland I'm not sure but it covers a multitude of sins*

OED (1753) 'dialect or slang'

FOZY adj. spongy, shrivelled, over-ripe

Norfolk (male, 1947, C1442/02003) *in my family we use Norfolk words like fozy which meant gone soft or mouldy like fruit and veg*

OED (1616) *fuzzy* 'obscure (except dialect)'; EDD *fozy* East Anglia

cf. BEETHY, DWINGEY, MAUMY

FROG AND TOAD n. road

London (male, 1949, C1442/00214) *frog and toad road use it quite frequently old English dying out*

OED (1859) 'rhyming slang (British and Australian)'

FUSHIONLESS adj. physically weak, lacking in stamina or energy

Aberdeen (female, 1958, C1442/01834) *fushionless it's a lovely word it means just having no strength at all*

DSL (1721) 'General Scots'

cf. FEMMER, PEELY-WALLY, SHILPIT

G

GALLOUS n. playboy, dandy

London (male, 1992, C1442/02728) *gallous a man who draws much female attention*

UD (2007)

GAMBOL n. forward roll

Birmingham (female, 1953, C1442/01543) *gambol which I didn't really think of being dialect until my daughter moved away from Birmingham and found that nobody ever knew it so it seemed to be a Birmingham word it means to do a somersault or a forward roll*

EDD West Midlands

cf. TISS UP

GANSEY n. sweater, jumper

Wolverhampton (male, 1947, C1442/00311) *my father came from Shropshire and he used to talk about a gansey which was a sweater or a cardigan living now in Cumbria I've heard people there talk about a gansey*

OED (1886) 'dialect variant of *Guernsey*'

GASH adj. rubbish, useless, superfluous

Cotswolds (female, 1991, C1442/02242) *gash meaning a little bit rubbish you know it's a bit poo*

OED (1937) 'slang (originally and chiefly nautical)'

cf. BOBBINS, JARG

GAWK vb. to gape, stare

Wolverhampton (female, 1981, C1442/01275) *gawk to stare don't know where it comes from an example would be 'that bloke was gawking at her'*

OED (1785) 'originally US or dialect'

GAZEBOED adj. drunk

Norwich (male, 1993, C1442/02015) *gazeboed means drunk*

DCS (c.2008)

cf. LARRUPED, MORTAL, SLIZZERED, STOCIOUS

GEMISCH n. fruit juice and sparkling water

London (female, 1976, C1442/00686) *gemisch it's used if somebody wants a soft drink or a fruit juice mixed with sparkling water my husband's German and it comes from Mischung which is a mixture*

GENNEL n. alleyway

Rotherham (female, 1938, C1442/00368) *gennel is a small passageway between houses just wide enough for walkers or cyclists*

Sheffield (male, 1965, C1442/01158) *gennel a passageway between two houses don't know where it's come from but regularly used*

OED (1613) 'dialect'

cf. BACK-JIGGER, GINNEL, JITTY, SNICKET, TWITCHEL, TWITTEN

GET WRONG vb. to be reprimanded, be told off

Wallsend (female, 1985, C1442/01677) *it means I'll get told off or I'll get into trouble so you say 'I'm not doing that or I'll get wrong' or 'don't do that or you'll get wrong*

A Dictionary of North East Dialect (Bill Griffiths, 2011); VOICES Sunderland (C1190/23/07) *we used to get wrong for saying knackered*

GIMP n. fool (used affectionately)

Norfolk (female, C1442/02039) *someone who is silly stupid someone who'd make a fool of themselves in public or act really giggly and stupid for no reason that's what we call a gimp*

OED (1924) 'slang (originally US)'

cf. BARMPOT, BUMBLEKLUTZ, BUMBOCLOT, DAFT/SOPPY HA'PORTH, EEJIT, NUMPTY, PLANK, TWONK, WAZZOCK, WUMPERT

GIP vb. to retch, gasp for air prior to vomiting

West Yorkshire (female, 1952, C1442/02641) *gip is from the West Riding of Yorkshire from the woollen district area it's a word to describe how you feel before you would be sick you might use it if you were not actually sick you would say 'I had something to eat and it made me gip' didn't actually make you sick but it's that feeling you're gonna be sick*

EDD Yorkshire

cf. BOKE, CHUNDER, HUGHIE

NOTES As with 'drunk', English has an extensive set of variants for 'vomit', as confirmed by several WordBank entries, and successive generations of students have ensured it remains a productive area of linguistic creativity. Alongside mainstream colloquial variants like *puke, spew* and *honk* the VOICES survey also noted regional variations on the theme of *throwing up* (e.g. *chucking up, hoying up, hurling* etc) and an impressive range of euphemistic expressions, from *pavement pizza* and *Technicolor yawn* to *praying on the great white telephone* or *driving the porcelain bus* [i.e. 'kneeling by the toilet']. I have a particular attachment to *gip*, though, as its similarity to the Leeds suburb of Gipton provided the basis for a phrase we used as students in Leeds in the 1980s: anyone who disappeared worse for wear during a night out was rather amusingly presumed to have *gone to Gipton*.

GINNEL n. alleyway

East Lancashire (male, 1986, C1442/02763) *we use the word ginnel to talk about a passage between terraced houses cobbled streets very narrow you would use that word above any other*

South Yorkshire (female, 1959, C1442/01283) *I mostly grew up in South Yorkshire and a word I quite savour now even though I don't live there any more is the word for a small passageway or a small lane which is ginnel I like the sound of that word and I don't hear it anywhere else*

West Yorkshire (female, 1953, C1442/01351) *I continue to use it even though I only lived in West Yorkshire for a very small part of my childhood a little passageway in between houses or buildings it's a ginnel*

West Yorkshire (female, 1987, C1442/00681) *ginnel a little alleyway that you can walk through when I try and use it in London people don't understand what I mean*

OED (1613) 'dialect'

cf. BACK-JIGGER, GENNEL, JITTY, SNICKET, TWITCHEL, TWITTEN

GOBSHITE n. good-for-nothing, ne'er-do-well

Stockport (male, 1945, C1442/01592) *my mother called me a gobshite I think it meant a lazy person who was in her bad books I've a feeling it's Irish but we're not of Irish descent*

OED (1948) 'chiefly Irish English'

GOPPING adj. physically unattractive, ugly

Manchester (female, 1970, C1442/01468) *in Manchester people say gopping that means really unattractive and I don't know where that comes from*

NPD (1991) *gopping* [= 'dirty'] 'Gulf War slang'; DCS *gopping* [= 'unattractive]

cf. BUTTERS, HOWFING, MINGING

GOOP n. drip, dullard

Eastbourne (male, 1943, C1442/02523) *my mother used to describe a drippy person or someone with not much intelligence as a bit of a goop that's from Eastbourne*

OED (1914) 'slang (originally US)'

GRAND adj. great, excellent

Ireland (male, 1964, C1442/02234) *grand in Irish dialect means great or wonderful or fine and it's that sense that I intend when I use it in conversation*

OED (1816) 'colloquial'

cf. BOSS, CANNY, CHAMPION, CUSHTY, LUSH, MINT, NANG, SICK, WICK

GROCKLE n. tourist

Cornwall (male, 1960, C1442/02695) *I grew up most of my life in Cornwall and we call people who are visitors grockles*

Yeovil (female, 1964, C1442/02760) *emmets happens to be a bit like grockles for tourists if you call them emmets or grockles it means you're not very happy with them and you wish they'd all go back home and leave you in peace it's like they're ants coming all over everything so that's why I like them words*

OED (1964) 'dialect and slang'

cf. EMMET

GROWLER n. waste-disposal unit

East Midlands (male, 1958, C1442/01020) *a family word for a waste-disposal unit the growler which has been handed on to our children and I suspect will be handed on to theirs as well*

GUDDLE vb. to rummage about

South Scotland (female, 1953, C1442/00977) *to rummage about it derives from guddling for fish I think and I would use it to guddle around in a bag or a handbag looking for something*

OED (1818) 'Scots'

cf. RATCH

GULLY n. large knife

Ashington (female, 1955, C1442/01340) *one of the words I would use which one of me friends the other day found very amusing was gully for knife usually a big knife like a bread knife as in 'pass us the gully so I can cut the stotty'*

OED (1592) 'Scots and north'

GURT adj. very, really

Bristol (female, 1981, C1442/00933) *gurt lush comes from Bristol it just means the best*

Somerset (male, 1972, C1442/02482) *gurt meaning great originating from the West of England is an abbreviation of the word great instead we say gurt*

EDD records *gurt* as localised spelling variant

cf. MAIN, WELL

GYP n. rough treatment, grief, verbal abuse

Goole (male, 1975, C1442/01211) *gyp meaning grief or stress 'she gave me a load of gyp'*

OED (1893) 'dialect or colloquial'

H

HAP vb. to wrap up (esp. for warmth)

Newcastle upon Tyne (female, 1931, C1442/01660) *we say hap yourself up against the cold that means wrap yourself up*

OED (c.1390) 'Irish and English regional (chiefly north)'

HAWM vb. to waste time, loiter

Grimsby (female, 1939, C1442/01378) *hawming about back of Doid's fishmeal factory down on the docks wasting time just drifting around*

OED (1847) 'dialect'

NOTES The verb *hawm* is known in this sense in several dialects, but the reference here to *back of Doid's* is particularly interesting as it echoes a VOICES contributor in Osgodby, Lincolnshire (C1190/21/03) who reports a similar phrase from her childhood: *your mam would say 'oh and why are you late home where you been' and if you dare you would've said 'I been egging back of Doid's'*. This type of folk idiom is extremely difficult to observe as it typically occurs in private or domestic exchanges, often in the form of stock phrases or habitual responses to everyday situations. In *A Prospect of Lincolnshire* (N. Field & A. White, 1984) John Widdowson lists several such folk expressions, including phrases used to describe natural phenomena (e.g. *the old lady is shaking her feather pillows out of her window* [= 'to snow']) which bring to mind the two WordBank contributions *black over Bill's mother's* and *enough blue sky to make a sailor a pair of trousers*. He also comments on traditional ways of deterring children who persist in asking annoying questions: a typical response to repeatedly being asked 'what's that' would be *a wimwam for meddler's noses* or *a wigwam for a mustard mill* or to 'where are we going?' might be *there and back to see how far it is*. My grandpa (born in Castleford 1906) had a particularly wide repertoire of stock responses and if ever we asked 'what's for tea?' would invariably reply *shit wi' sugar on* (or *nibb-its* if we had company). I recently stumbled across a Facebook discussion group of similarly aged northerners united by fond memories of *shit wi' sugar on* and a single reference at UD (2010).

HEAD LIKE A ROBBER'S DOG adj. unkempt, scruffy (of hair)

Liverpool (male, 1964, C1442/01498) *got a head like a robber's dog it means your hair isn't very tidy at all I've no idea where the actual phrase comes from but it's certainly used in Liverpool*

GDS (1959) *head like a robber's dog* [= 'ugly']

HOGGIN n. pudding

London (female, 1985, C1442/02640) *we have family words that we made up for pudding we say hoggin so we say 'mum what's for hoggin'*

EDD *hoggan* [= 'pasty']

HOT adj. physically attractive

Barnet (female, 1993, C1442/01094) *beaut it means attractive and I would use it when I see a hot guy I would say 'he's a beaut'*

OED (1926) 'slang (originally US)'

cf. BOOM-TING, BUFF (TING), PENG, TICK

HOWFING adj. physically unattractive, ugly

Scottish Borders (male, 1974, C1442/01796) *howfing means unattractive I've no idea where it comes from*

OED (1583) *howfing* [= 'clumsy, awkward'] 'Scottish'; DSL (1584) *howfing* [= 'shabby, beggarly looking']

cf. BUTTERS, GOPPING, MINGING

HUGHIE vb. to vomit

London (female, 1986, C1442/00612) *hughie means to be sick and I think it comes from the sound you make when you vomit so you could say 'that person is making me want to hughie'*

NPD (1985) 'Scotland'

cf. BOKE, CHUNDER, GIP

I

I'M A SHOE phr. 'I miss you'

Norfolk (female, 1986, C1442/02086) *me and my friends use the term I'm a shoe instead of I miss you because when you pair up you can make a pair of shoes and it's quite a sweet really nice thing to say to each other and it caught on and got bigger and bigger so that people are using it that we don't know*

UD (2009) records *mishou* in this sense

INTERPEST vb. to interrupt

Stockport (male, 1964, C1442/01957) *in my family my sister made up a word inadvertently interpest which is to make a pest of yourself by interrupting since she accidentally said it we use it frequently and it's a useful word*

J

JAM vb. to press firm by treading, flatten

Norfolk (male, 1947, C1442/02003) *to jam on was to trample or squash down as in 'someone's been a-jamming on it'*

OED (1787) 'dialect'

JARG adj. rubbish, poor quality, fake

Liverpool (female, 1993, C1442/00175) *jarg which means something is rubbish or fake as in 'oh this film is jarg' or 'look at his jarg bag'*

UD (2004)

cf. BOBBINS, GASH

JIFFLE vb. to fidget, wriggle

Lincolnshire (female, 1988, C1442/02210) *jiffle means to fidget or wriggle around you'd say 'stop jiffling'*

OED (1674) 'dialect'

JIGGERED adj. exhausted, tired out

Durham (female, 1961, C1442/01810) *in my family somebody would say 'I'm jiggered' and that would mean you were exhausted or really tired*

OED (1862) 'dialect and slang'

cf. FANNAKAPANNED, CASSENED, WABBIT

JIMMY SQUIGGLE n. wee, visit to toilet

Yorkshire (female, 1987, C1442/01143) *one word that I use between friends and family is Jimmy Squiggle so if you really need the loo if you need a wee you say 'oh I'm just going for a Jimmy Squig' it's a phrase that we find funny and I think is laughed at as well amongst my sisters don't know where it comes from a naval term I believe my mum's dad was in the Navy and I think it's come down the line from that and we use it whenever I go back home or to my sisters I say 'oh I'm just gonna squidge a Jimmy' and then new phrases come from that just the way the word order gets played around with or just 'going over for a Jimmy Squiggle'*

OED (1937) *Jimmy Riddle* [= 'rhyming slang for *piddle*']

JITTY n. alleyway

Market Harborough (female, C1442/00295) *I love the word jitty when we moved to Market Harborough in Leicestershire four years ago it was a word I'd never heard but it's in local usage it means alleyway walkway path and jitty I think is wonderful*

Middleton Cheney (male, 1961, C1442/00123) *jitty meaning alleyway*

Nottinghamshire (male, 1944, C1442/00295) *twitchel which means the footpath between houses and in Leicester that footpath is referred to as a jitty or a jetty*

EDD, SED & VOICES Midlands

cf. BACK-JIGGER, GENNEL, GINNEL, SNICKET, TWITCHEL, TWITTEN

JOKES adj. funny, amusing; phr. expression used to comment (esp. sarcastically) on something amusing

London (male, 1992, C1442/00666) *when something's bare funny you go 'LMAO' and it means laughing my arse off so if someone says something funny you go 'LMAO' it's bare jokes*

London (female, C1442/00398) *some people in London say jokes if you're laughing about something*

Reading (female, 1995, C1442/00955) *chunder means be sick and throw up but it's quite humorous because there was this video on YouTube that went global about some person and the gap year and it was really funny and it's evolved and become part of every day speech it's usually used in connotations of drinking too much so you'd go out and then you'd chunder because you were drunk rather than necessarily because you were ill but it's quite a jokes word*

South East (female, 1992, C1442/01092) *something that we say is quite shameful actually is it's well jokes I heard initially in year nine so I must've been about thirteen fourteen and I thought it was a really weird thing to say 'cause you might as well just say 'it's funny' it means that something's funny so 'well jokes'*

GDS (2005) 'UK black'

K

KECKS n. trousers

Liverpool (female, 1941, C1442/00538) *kecks is a Liverpool word for men's trousers*

Liverpool (male, 1958, C1442/00979) *I haven't heard many other people use kecks but it means trousers*

OED (1900) 'British slang and regional (chiefly north and Scotland)'

KELTERMAN n. night soil man, gong-farmer

Cumbria (male, 1942, C1442/00513) *kelterman somebody who picks up the night soil*

OED [1847] *kelter* [= 'rubbish'] 'dialect'; EDD *kelter(ment)* [= 'rubbish, waste']

KETS n. sweets

Darlington (female, 1983, C1442/00863) *kets I would use with my friends to describe sweets*

UD [2004]

KINKHOST n. whooping cough

London (female, 1943, C1442/00104) *my grandparents and my aunts in the north of Scotland used to talk about the kinkhost for coughs which I know Dutch neighbours could understand*

OED (1584) 'obscure (except Scotland)'

L

LADGE vb. to embarrass, humiliate

Scarborough (female, 1981, C1442/01200) *ladging it's from York and it means something embarrassing or something unpleasant*

Romani Rokkeripen To-Divvus (Thomas Acton & Donald Kenrick, 1984) *ladge* [= 'to shame'], *ladged* [= 'ashamed']; UD [2004] *ladge* [= 'to embarrass']

IStock Photo

LAKE vb. to play

Cumbria (male, 1942, C1442/00513) *laking means playing*

Holmfirth (female, C1442/01757) *I'm from Holmfirth but I've moved to Sheffield but a word that I use a lot'd be laking which I think is a Nordic word which means to mess about to play with so I'd say to my mates 'what you laking at?'*

South Yorkshire (female, 1983, C1442/01962) *my phrase is 'art thou laking out' which translates in Yorkshire to are you playing out it's something that when you are younger and you're going to your friend's house and you knock on the door and they come to the door and you say 'are you laking out?' and it means are you coming out to play*

OED (c.1300) 'now chiefly dialect'

LAKES adj. mad, crazy

Longford (male, 1986, C1442/02608) *lakes means to go crazy or to have fun it comes from friends in Longford where I'm from to use it in a sentence 'I went lakes last night' or 'the party was lakes' it's a funny phrase used a bit in Longford and other areas but wouldn't be all over Ireland*

OED (1934) 'slang'

LARRUPED adj. drunk

Sheffield (male, 1965, C1442/01158) *well larruped meaning drunk*

DCS (c.2000)

cf. GAZEBOED, MORTAL, SLIZZERED, STOCIOUS

IStock Photo

LERRUPS n. tatters, rags

Cornwall (male, 1985, C1442/00790) *lerrups I'm from North Cornwall and it's used quite widely round there the most common context is all to lerrups which means all to pot all messed up disorganised but people also use it to mean ruined as in destroyed physically so I've heard people say a broken down car has been lashed to lerrups so overused as well I suppose*

EDD Devon and Cornwall

LIKE CHEESE AT FOURPENCE phr. to look lost, loiter, be stood up

Grimsby (female, 1939, C1442/01378) *sitting there like cheese at fourpence was a phrase we used to use to describe people who were looking rather silly and lost this might have come from across the border from Yorkshire into Lancashire I'm not sure it's something that we used a lot at home*

wiktionary.org *like cheese at fourpence* [= 'to wait idly, timewaste'] Lancashire

NOTES This appears to be a Lancashire term used to poke fun at someone useless or deemed to be making no useful contribution to a given activity and further proof of how inventive we are with terms for personality traits we view with contempt or amusement – witness the number of terms submitted to the WordBank for 'fool'. We have several colloquial phrases to express the same sentiment: OED (1972) records *waste of space* and NPD (1978) *neither use nor ornament. Like cheese at fourpence*, however, reminds me of a comparable expression I have only ever heard my wife use: *sat there like piffy*. A couple of entries at UD (2004) suggest that slightly longer variants *sat there like piffy on a wet weekend* or *like piffy on a rock bun* are known in Manchester, while an online discussion thread at wordreference.com suggests *sat there like piffy on a rock bun* is common in the Peak District (my wife comes from Ashbourne). Another well-known slang term recorded in GDS (2001) confirms the pleasure we all take in dismissing someone who is *as useless as a one-legged man in an arse-kicking contest.*

LMAO excl. phrase used to express amusement or hilarity

London (male, 1992, C1442/00666) *when something's bare funny you go 'LMAO' and it means laughing my arse off so if someone says something funny you go 'LMAO' it's bare jokes*

UD (2002)

NOTES The advent of text speak, online communication and social media is considered by some observers to have had potentially the greatest impact on English – albeit principally on written English – since the introduction of the printing press in the 15th century. As the technology has only been available for a few years it is probably too early to say whether the innovations it has prompted will endure, particularly as devices and platforms change so swiftly. In the early days of text messages people were restricted to a limited number of characters (as is true of Twitter today), so inevitably abbreviations and shorthand were widely adopted to allow greater flexibility. Certain texting conventions emerged very quickly, such as omitting redundant letters (e.g. *thnx* [= 'thanks']) or using single letters and numbers to represent whole words or combinations of letters and numbers to represent English phonemes (e.g. *u* [= 'you'], *4* [= 'for'] and *cul8er* [= 'see you later']). This type of adaptation has been common

IStock Photo

practice for longer than we might imagine – we all use a variety of universal and personalised abbreviations to write lists and make notes, for instance, and in 1867 US author Charles Carroll Bombaugh published a collection of poems and word games including 'Essay to Miss Catharine Jay' which features the line *I wrote 2 U B 4* – a visual pun that predates mobile phones by some 125 years. This kind of orthographic modification has no effect on spoken language as *to* and *2, you* and the letter *U* etc. are pronounced identically by speakers of most varieties of English regardless of how they spell them.

On the other hand the use of acronyms in texting (e.g. *lol* [= 'lots of love' or, more commonly, 'laughing out loud'], *lmao* [= 'laughing my ass/arse off'] and *rofl* [= 'rolling on the floor laughing']) has produced some interesting linguistic quirks. As is the case with acronyms in conventional English (e.g. *NATO, BBC* and *CD-ROM*) some text acronyms are pronounced as if they were words (e.g. *lol* is pronounced to rhyme with 'doll'), some as individual letters (e.g. *omg* = 'oh my God' is pronounced 'oh emm gee'), or a combination of both (e.g. *btw* = 'by the way' is generally pronounced 'bee-tee-dubz' and often used by younger speakers to introduce a statement or to add emphasis). The first type is particularly interesting as in spoken discourse speakers can derive adjectives, create plural forms or conjugate them as if they were regular verbs, so you hear people saying *she lolled her head off* or *we were lolling for ages*.

LOUP vb. to leap, jump

Newcastle upon Tyne (female, 1931, C1442/01660) *Geordie horses and sheep can loup over fences*

OED (c.1480) 'Scottish'

LUBELL vb. to commit adultery

Middleton Cheney (male, 1961, C1442/00123) *lubelling is basically committing adultery really playing around and it's a phrase that certainly old folk use and younger people use it as well*

OED (1831) *lowbell* [= 'to condemn/humiliate publicly for inappropriate behaviour']; EDD records *lubell* as localised spelling variant

LUG n. knot, tangle (in hair)

Birmingham (female, 1977, C1442/00057) *when I was growing up in Birmingham we used to use the word lug or luggy I don't hear it at all where I live in Swansea it means knots in your hair so a lug is a knot and luggy is knotty*

EDD & SED North and West Midlands

cf. CLIT

LUSH adj. great, excellent

Bath (female, 1971, C1442/02730) *in the West Country anything good is lush but if you describe green grass as lush that could lead to a little bit of misunderstanding*

Bristol (female, 1981, C1442/00933) *gurt lush comes from Bristol it just means the best* OED (1928)

cf. BOSS, CANNY, CHAMPION, CUSHTY, GRAND, MINT, NANG, SICK, WICK

M

MADE-UP adj. pleased

Barnet (female, C1442/02420) *in Merseyside where I live now people will say they are made-up about something that means they're very pleased about something that isn't a term I think people would use at all in the South East I come from Barnet North London and I don't think I would ever have heard it there*

OED (1946) 'Irish English and English regional (esp. Liverpool)'

MAFT vb. to be stiflingly hot

East Yorkshire (female, 1960, C1442/00784) *it's enough to maft you means it's very hot and I think it's from around Hull and Beverley area*

EDD *maft* [= 'to be stifled or overpowered by want of air or great heat'] Yorkshire

IStock Photo

MAIN adv. very, really

Wiltshire (male, 1951, C1442/02711) *main as in 'that's main big' 'main happy' meaning very I just know it from childhood from Wiltshire*

OED (1632)

cf. GURT, WELL

MAM n. mother

County Durham (female, 1981, C1442/00967) *up north we say mam not mum*

Eaglescliffe (female, 1962, C1442/00083) *when we talk about family we talk about our mam our dad*

Hull (female, 1998, C1442/00590) *me mam it means your mum or summat like that*

OED (1570) 'British colloquial and regional'

MANDI DON'T KNOW WHAT THE BUER'S ROKKERING phr. I don't know what the woman is talking about

Newark (female, 1969, C1442/01079) *a phrase and saying that only people from Newark would know mandi don't know what the buer's rokkering and what that means is I don't know what the woman is talking about*

OED (1807) *buer* [= 'woman'] 'northern dialect and tramps' slang'; OED (1856) *rokker* [= 'to speak, understand'] 'cant or Romani'

NOTES There have been occasional attempts to document Anglo-Romani and *Romani Rokkeripen To-Divvus* (Thomas Acton and Donald Kenrick, 1984) records *mandi* [= 'I'], *buer* [= 'woman'] and *rokker* [= 'to talk, speak']. Given the presence of traveller communities on the fringes of British society it is perhaps not surprising that very few words have entered mainstream usage but Romani has influenced local dialects in many parts of the country. Speakers either side of the English–Scottish border, for instance, will be familiar with terms like *gadgie* [from *gaujo* = '(non-gypsy) man'], *minge* [from *minj* = 'female genitals'], *mort* [= 'girl, woman'], *mooey* [from *mui* = 'mouth, face'], *radgie* [from *radge* = 'mad, angry'] and *scran* [= 'food']. A small set of Romani words are used more widely, including *cushty* [from *kushti* = 'good'], *mullered* [= 'dead, killed'] and *mush* [= 'man (esp. as form of address']. Probably the most unfortunate contribution of Anglo-Romani is the word *chav*, which in recent years has been adopted by young speakers all over the country to refer negatively to a stereotypical young ne'er-do-well characterised by cheap designer clothes, anti-social behaviour and low social status. The word derives from the much more endearing Anglo-Romani word *chavvi* [= 'boy, son'] and illustrates how certain social groups have unfortunately always attracted suspicion and condemnation. A WordBank contributor (C1442/02355) from the Medway, Kent who claims to *pukker* [= 'to speak] Romani, for instance, says he will often *jel down the tober to see my little chavvis in my vardo* ['go down the road to see my children in my caravan'].

MARDY adj. moody, sullen, spoilt (esp. of child)

Ashby-de-la-Zouch (male, 1986, C1442/01473) *being grumpy and grouchy but more stroppy than that like a four-year-old throwing a paddy and mardy weather is overcast cold and rainy*

Burton upon Trent (male, 1946, C1442/00343) *an adjective I used as a boy and I don't hear anywhere else but in the East Midlands mardy refers to a boy who's being miserable and whining someone for example who would take his cricket set home 'cause he didn't want to play any more*

IStock Photo

Coventry (female, 1940, C1442/01800) *someone usually a child who is in a bad temper and sulking*

Doncaster (male, 1949, C1442/00559) *if a younger child is not happy you'd say it was mardy*

East Midlands (male, 1958, C1442/01020) *mardy which we used to use at school a lot which meant bad-tempered sulky reluctant and difficult*

East Midlands (female, 1975, C1442/02491) *mardy it means when you're not very happy or you're grumpy or irritable and I don't know where it's from*

Grimsby (female, 1939, C1442/01378) *a child in a bad temper and grumpy*

Leicester (female, 1977, C1442/02502) *when I was child I thought that everybody said mardy and I remember one day not knowing how to spell it so I tried to look it up in the dictionary and was slightly concerned that I couldn't find it thinking the dictionary must be wrong until I realised that mardy was a slang word from the area in which I live having now lived all over the country I don't tend to use mardy very often any more but whenever I do you can either see the blankness on people's face or if they nod you know you're talking to someone usually from the Midlands often particularly from Leicester and some sort of bond occurs just because of a simple word like mardy which basically means grumpy disgruntled irritable*

Leicestershire (male, 1974, C1442/01209) *mardy meaning broken or upset generally out of sorts someone can be mardy so they can be a bit grumpy or very upset a machine can be mardy so it won't be working the computer can be mardy Leicestershire word probably East Midlands when I went to university no one knew what I was talking about and they said I used it quite often which was a surprise to me*

Lincolnshire (female, 1963, C1442/01375) *cross or sullen or bad-tempered usually applied to a teenager*

Nottingham (female, 1985, C1442/00128) *mardy in the Midlands means bad-tempered or if you're annoyed about something it could be said that you're mardy*

Nottingham (female, 1947, C1442/01076) *mardy sulky what you do if you don't get your own way 'oh she's being really mardy today'*

Nottingham (female, 1937, C1442/01880) *tearful and always moaning and unable to stand any sort of pain*

Nottinghamshire (male, 1944, C1442/00295) *mardy from Nottingham which is usually referring to a sullen or bad-tempered child*

Nottinghamshire (male, 1959, C1442/01353) *mardy easily upset whingeing about trivial things*

South Yorkshire (female, 1959, C1442/01283) *a word that we used a lot as children growing up was mardy when somebody was generally in a bad mood and moaning or grumbling and I think that's a great descriptive word mardy*

OED (1874) 'regional, chiefly north'

cf. CARNAPTIOUS, MAUNGY

NOTES The sheer number of contributors who wanted to ensure *mardy* was included in the WordBank testifies to the continued vitality of this much-loved dialect term. Several contributors claimed it is exclusively a Leicester word or only used in Nottingham, but it clearly occurs over a wide area of the North and Midlands, and is particularly well established in the East Midlands. D.H. Lawrence refers to a *mard-arsed kid* in his 1928 poem 'The Collier's Wife' and *mardy* crops up frequently in Alan Sillitoe's 1958 novel *Saturday Night and Sunday Morning*, set in Nottingham. Perhaps more impressively you will hear youngsters all over the world singing along to Arctic Monkeys' 2004 single 'Mardy Bum', meaning this 19th-century Midlands dialect word now enjoys international currency.

MARGE n. mother

East London (female, 1993, C1442/00535) *marge I guess that comes from Marge Simpson but yeah your marge is your mum*

UD (2007)

cf. MAM

MASH vb. to make/brew tea

Coventry (female, 1948, C1442/01267) *mash the tea meant that the tea was brewing and was fairly common in Coventry*

OED (1845) 'British regional'

IStock Photo

MAUMY adj. soft, overcooked

Leicester (female, 1957, C1442/01381) *maumy is used when you boil potatoes too long and they go soft they say they've gone maumy or they've maumed down I learnt that when I first started work from an older woman probably born in the 1920s in Leicester*

OED (1691) 'English regional (chiefly north)'; EDD *maumy* [= 'soft, tasteless (of food)']

cf. BEETHY, DWINGEY, FOZY

MAUNGY adj. miserable, moody, sullen

Sheffield (female, 1962, C1442/01550) *maungy means miserable*

EDD (1865) North

cf. CARNAPTIOUS, MARDY

MEEKIN vb. to dither, suffer from indecisiveness

Northamptonshire (female, 1979, C1442/01103) *a word I use with my friends that means dithering being indecisive not making a decision it comes from a school friend of one of my friends it was her surname and she was indecisive and that's why there is a group of about ten to fifteen people who will say 'stop meekining' when you're being indecisive*

cf. SWITHER

MENTAL adj. exciting, surprising, mind-blowing

Lancashire (female, 1935, C1442/01980) *I think I use the phrase 'that's mental' a lot which means something's surprising or unexpected I think it's come from school days where being excited meant you were going mental going crazy*

NPD (1998)

MINCH n. joker, tease

South East (male, 1991, C1442/00336) *minch I think it's an internet-based thing it's a light-hearted insult so if someone has a little joke at you you go 'oh well done you minch' sarcastically just as a little insult if you're actually angry with someone you wouldn't use it it's more of a jokey phrase a little casual banter it's sort of like 'oh you joker' but if you want to put them down for getting you sort of thing*

UD (2011)

MINGER n. physically unattractive person

London (female, C1442/00465) *if someone's unattractive we just say 'he's a bit of a minger' that's an old-fashioned one now*

London (female, C1442/00398) *some people in London use minger to say ugly*

London Nigerian (female, 1996, C1442/00410) *butters means that you're really ugly it's basically a minger but butters is worse*

OED (1992) 'British slang'

MINGING adj. dirty, smelly, disgusting, (and, by extension) physically unattractive, ugly

Chelsea (female, 1994, C1442/00344) *when someone's unattractive minging*

Gateshead (female, 1957, C1442/01613) *minging it means horrible dirty nasty I don't know where it comes from and it wasn't a very nice word until recently and then it seems to have been accepted into general use in the North East it's not something that you want to be called*

Glasgow (male, 1983, C1442/00600) *minging means unattractive 'that person over there is totally minging'*

London (female, C1442/00535) *for unattractive minging*

Scotland (female, 1942, C1442/00485) *unattractive is minging*

OED (1970) *minging* [= 'smelly'] 'slang (originally Scottish)'; NPD (1985) *minging* [= 'unattractive'] 'Scotland'; VOICES confirms both senses

cf. RONKING

MINT adj. great, excellent

Bedfordshire (male, C1442/02363) *mint originally from the North of England it's a term I've used for coming up to ten years now for something that's extremely good excellent satisfying 'that's mint'*

GDS (1989) 'Canadian/US/UK teen'

cf. BOSS, CANNY, CHAMPION, CUSHTY, LUSH, MINT, NANG, SICK, WICK

MITCH vb. to play truant

Cardiff (female, 1968, C1442/02644) *mitch means to play truant you'd use it in the expression 'he mitched off school' I don't know where it comes from but they use it in the valleys of South Wales and in Cardiff*

South Devon (female, 1975, C1442/00788) *in Devon we use mitching for playing truant*

Swansea (male, 1941, C1442/01522) *to play truant we would call it mitching I don't know where it comes from*

OED (1580) 'British regional and Irish English'

cf. TWAG, WAG

MITHER vb. to bother, pester, annoy

Coventry (female, 1948, C1442/01267) *when I was growing up my mother used to say mithered and we took this to mean she was very flustered and couldn't concentrate*

North West (male, 1957, C1442/02435) *mither is widespread in the North West and seems to mean to irritate or harass as in 'oh stop mithering me'*

South (male, 1959, C1442/01066) *I'm really a southerner living in Manchester but some of the words they use I quite enjoy one word is to mither somebody so 'don't mither me' don't bother me so I sometimes use that phrase and of course if you use it in the south nobody understands what you mean*

OED (1847) 'regional (northern and midland)'

cf. BUSSLE, CHAUVE, MOITHER

MOITHER vb. to bother, pester, annoy

London (female, 1978, C1442/02450) *I really like the word moithered it's not from my dialect I think it's from Yorkshire dialect but I've heard someone from Wales who thinks it's from North Wales as well it means bothered or flustered by somebody else I really like it because although it's about being bothered it sounds really gentle*

OED (1860) 'Irish English, Manx English & English regional (northern and midland)'

cf. BUSSLE, CHAUVE, MITHER

MOOLAH n. money

London (female, 1994, C1442/01263) *moolah for money commonly used with friends I wouldn't use it with parents or teachers so if I have a lot of moolah you have a lot of money*

OED (1937) 'slang (originally US)'

cf. BUNCE

MORTAL adj. extremely drunk

Newcastle upon Tyne (female, 1994, C1442/01680) *another word for drunk is absolutely mortal*

OED (1796) 'English regional (north)'

cf. GAZEBOED, LARRUPED, SLIZZERED, STOCIOUS

N

NANG adj. great, excellent

London (female, C1442/02685) *nang means good*

NPD (2004)

cf. BOSS, CANNY, CHAMPION, CUSHTY, LUSH, MINT, SICK, WICK

NESH adj. weak, susceptible to cold

Burton upon Trent (male, 1946, C1442/00343) *as a boy nesh was used quite a lot and I think it's cognate with nice it means someone who for example won't go out in the snow 'cause it's too cold or won't go swimming because the water's too deep*

Burton upon Trent (male, 1964, C1442/02453) *we use the word nesh meaning somebody that feels the cold too much if somebody wants to turn the fire up you say 'what are you nesh?' it's an old English word meaning weak*

IStock Photo

Chesterfield (female, 1989, C1442/00457) *nesh is a brilliant word it means to not like the cold or the wet to be a bit weak and wimpy and a bit you know just nesh it's very difficult to describe it's something my mum uses she's from Manchester originally*

Derby (female, 1949, C1442/01237) *I like the word nesh I first heard it in Derby and it means being a bit sensitive to the cold not very hardy so you might say 'oh you're a bit nesh' if someone's moaning about being cold*

Grimsby (female, 1950, C1442/00038) *nesh I believe to be Sheffield as in somebody who is a bit of a wimp*

Leicestershire (male, 1956, C1442/01124) *nesh I've never seen it written but we used to use it to describe someone who was very sensitive to the cold but by extension we called someone nesh who was feeble a weakling in general*

Newark (female, 1983, C1442/00420) *in Newark there's a word nesh and it means cold so I'd probably say 'oh it's a bit nesh today'*

Nottingham (female, 1951, C1442/01093) *nesh is a word that's quite local to Nottingham and it means being a bit whingey a bit sort of weedy being cold when you shouldn't be cold really*

Nottinghamshire (male, 1944, C1442/00295) *nesh which means sensitive to cold in particular and perhaps sensitive to pain generally which is quite a nice word because I don't know of any proper English word which is equivalent to nesh*

Sheffield (female, 1951, C1442/01308) *nesh it means that you don't like the cold*

South West England (female, 1934, C1442/00440) *one of my favourite words is nesh which was a word my grandmother used to mean not very strong rather frail and collapsible rather like a lettuce so people were described as nesh if they spent too much time indoors and didn't play healthy outdoor games*

Wakefield (female, 1980, C1442/01497) *my mum when she's cold calls herself nesh she says 'am I being nesh or is it cold' it means a bit cold a bit weedy a bit pathetic I'm not sure where it comes from it's maybe a Yorkshire thing*

OED (1230) 'now English regional (chiefly north), rare'; VOICES Swanwick, Derbyshire (C1190/14/02) *if you kept your coat on in the house people'd say you want to take that off you won't feel the benefit you'll be nesh*

NITHERED adj. cold, freezing

North Yorkshire (female, 1966, C1442/01571) *you know when you've been out and it's cold and it's wet and you come in and you're freezing but you're not just cold you're cold right through to your bones that's the word nithered I come in and 'oh I'm nithered' and you want to get under a blanket with a nice hot water bottle and a cup of tea*

OED (1691) 'Scottish and English regional (north)'

cf. DERBY (ROAD), PARKY, TATERS, THANDA

NO HANDSELS excl. phrase used to avoid unpopular or unwanted task

UK (female, C1442/02387) *when I was a child if somebody threw a ball up in the air and we thought it was going to go over a wall and it might get lost there would be a cry of 'no handsels' meaning I'm not going to be responsible for it*

OED (1605) records *handsel* [= 'to use for first time, to be first to test']

NOTES *The Lore and Language of Schoolchildren* (Peter & Iona Opie, 1959) records common phrases used by children for 'claiming precedence' – e.g. staking claim to be the first to have a go at skipping or the first to bat in a game of cricket. Among the most popular phrases documented by the Opies were variations on the terms *bagsy go first* or *me foggy*. I have certainly heard my own children (aged between 13 and 19) use *bagsy* but to claim the most comfortable chair or first choice of sweet or chocolate they more frequently use *shotgun*. Children's language and lore is a rich resource for linguists and the subtle codes governed by terms like *shotgun* can seem impenetrable to adults. My children and their friends apply a sliding scale whereby an initial claim of *shotgun* can be 'trumped' by someone shouting *shotgun reload* as long as they do so within a split second of hearing the first claim of *shotgun*. This second claim can in turn be overridden by an immediate cry of *jedi*, although this inevitably disintegrates into an argument over who said what first and how quickly. The Opies also explored terms for 'avoidance' – i.e. justifying not having to do the washing-up or not having to fetch a ball that has been kicked, hit or thrown over the garden fence. The two most common recorded for avoiding unpleasant tasks are *bagsy not me* and *fains I*. There is no mention of *no handsels*, but the OED entry does perhaps offer a hint of how this word might be applied in the context of children's play. The term *fains I* even made an appearance in the 2012 *Downton Abbey* Christmas Special when under-butler Thomas Barrow, keen to avoid being the bearer of bad news to his intimidating superior, delivered the line *fains I tell Mr Carson*.

NUMPTY n. fool (used affectionately)

Ayrshire (female, 1969, C1442/00222) *numpty would really mean someone who was a bit of a fool so if you'd done something wrong you would go 'oh you were a bit of a numpty there' I think it's quite colloquial from the West Coast of Scotland but maybe other people in other areas have used it before I think it's becoming a wee bit more well-known*

NPD (1911) 'Scottish'

cf. BARMPOT, BUMBLEKLUTZ, BUMBOCLOT, DAFT/SOPPY HA'PORTH, EEJIT, GIMP, PLANK, TWONK, WAZZOCK, WUMPERT

O

OMGWTF excl. phrase used to express surprise, incredulity or embarrassment

Surrey (female, 1988, C1442/02732) *OMGWTF meaning oh my God what the fuck it probably comes from American TV programmes in recent years*

OED (1917) *OMG* 'colloquial'; OED (1985) *WTF*; UD (2003) *OMGWTF*

ON THE BOX adj. off work, on sick leave

Walsall (male, 1985, C1442/01497) *on the box when people are off sick from work and being paid when they're signed off by the doctor as they have a sick note or a doctor's note*

Black Country Dialect (Brendan Hawthorne, 2013)

NOTES Intriguingly until relatively recently this phrase seems to have escaped the attention of dialect dictionaries despite numerous glossaries of Black Country English. When I mentioned this phrase to my *mom* [= 'mother' in the West Midlands] she knew what it meant instantly, but then she did grow up in Caldmore, Walsall. Further confirmation is provided by an anecdote recorded in VOICES Dudley (C1190/05/02): *I said 'ah I'm on the box' he says 'well can you explain what that is' I says 'I'm on the sick' then there was like all these puzzled looks.*

ON THE HUH adj. not straight, askew

Norfolk (female, 1982, C1442/02165) *one of the words I use is on the huh which is a Norfolk phrase and you use it if something's not quite straight you could say it's on the huh*

East Anglia (female, 1962, C1442/01916) *something is not straight it's falling over so for example a shelf on a wall isn't straight or picture isn't hung level so that's on the huh*

EDD East Anglia

ON TO PLUMS adj. unlucky, unfortunate

West Scotland (female, 1960, C1442/00904) *you're on to plums which means you are unfortunate you're out of luck it's not gonna happen I think it may have come from fruit machines from plums coming up and not paying out any cash*

OOSE n. fluff

London (female, 1985, C1442/02640) *oose is a word that means fluff on a jacket or piece of clothing so we say 'there's a bit of oose on that jacket'*

South Scotland (female, C1442/00990) *oose means fluff usually talking about fluff under a bed which gathers and hasn't been cleaned or if your clothing is covered in lint then you say it's oosie covered in fluff*

OED (1822) 'Scots variant of *wool*'

OUT-LAW n. parent of long-term (unmarried) partner

London (female, 1939, C1442/01421) *out-law I hear used for people who are not in-laws because people have not legally married but they use out-law to describe their mother-in-law or father-in-law*

UD (2004) *out-law* [= 'parent of long-term unmarried partner']; UD (2006) *out-law* [= 'parent of ex-partner']; UD (2008) *out-law* [= 'live-in partner of sibling']

OWT pron. anything

Leeds (female, 1998, C1442/01158) *sometimes I say 'oh d'you want owt' which means do you want anything and I think that's Yorkshire*

OED (c.1000) 'now regional (chiefly north)

NOTES The words *owt* [= 'anything] and its counterpart *nowt* [= 'nothing'] are well-known markers of northern dialect, widely associated with local speech in Yorkshire, Lancashire and elsewhere. A personal bugbear is the widespread belief that they are universally pronounced to rhyme with 'out', an impression reinforced in recent years by the successful advertising campaign for Allinson wholemeal bread – *the bread wi' nowt taken out* – a catchy slogan but only if *nowt* rhymes with *out*. Having spent my early childhood in Pontefract and retaining a strong affinity with West Yorkshire I still use *owt* and *nowt* (albeit knowingly) but always pronounce them to rhyme with 'oat' and 'note' – a pronunciation that characterises local speech in much of Derbyshire, Staffordshire, Nottinghamshire, Yorkshire and Lancashire. There are indeed pockets of the country – notably Manchester, Middlesbrough and Newcastle upon Tyne – where they rhyme with 'out' but a rhyme with 'oat' arguably has a wider distribution. This important distinction was demonstrated in an episode of the ITV soap *Coronation Street* in

March 2014 when in one scene Kylie Platt (played by Paula Lane from Hebden Bridge, Yorkshire) said *well first of all technically it's mine and David's house and secondly we've nowt* [pronounced 'note'] *worth nicking bar the telly and a box of Lego*. Minutes later Eva Price (played by Catherine Tyldesley from Walkden, Greater Manchester) said *I can't believe you Leanne you knew me mum was leaving and you never said owt* [pronounced 'out']. The word *owt* also occurs regularly pronounced as 'oat' in the VOICES survey, with examples in Mansfield (C1190/21/03) *owt above Watford Gap's north isn't it*; Barrow-in-Furness (C1190/11/01) *that's what they learnt me straightaway not hello thank you please sorry where's the toilet owt like that they just learnt me my swear-words*; Castleford (C1190/19/01) *I never ever stole owt I never pinched owt in my life I never went into a shop and pinched owt*; and Cleethorpes (C1190/16/01) *I don't really go out drinking or owt like that if I go out it's usually bike BMXing or summat like that*.

OXTER n. armpit

Glasgow (female, 1956, C1442/01297) *oxter would mean medical speak axilla or armpit*

London (female, 1943, C1442/00104) *my grandparents and my aunts in the north of Scotland used to talk about oxters for armpits*

OED (1420) 'English regional (north, Scottish, Irish and Manx English'

P

PADDY, THROW A vb. to be in a bad mood, have a temper tantrum

Ashby-de-la-Zouch (male, 1986, C1442/01473) *being grumpy and grouchy but more stroppy than that like a four-year-old throwing a paddy*

OED (1894) 'colloquial'

cf. COB ON

PANSHITE n. state of agitation, panic

Hartlepool (female, 1964, C1442/02498) *panshite it's from Hartlepool North East generally it means to get yourself into an agitated state as in 'I couldn't work out what to do I got meself into a real panshite'*

EDD (1895)

cf. PUCKATERRY, TWO AND EIGHT

PAR vb. to ignore, snub

North London (male, 1986, C1442/00595) *par is a term that is used to mean to dismiss someone so if someone called me and I didn't pick up their phone call it means I'm parring them or if someone asks you a question and you don't answer them it's a par so it's a form of disrespect when you dismiss someone grime artists from East London started using the word par and I'm from North London but all of a sudden over the last year we've been using that term as well*

DCS (2009) 'multi-ethnic youth slang'

PARKY adj. cold, chilly

Sheffield (female, 1951, C1442/01308) *parky means it is cold*

OED (1895) 'slang'

cf. DERBY (ROAD), NITHERED, TATERS, THANDA

PARMO n. dish of meat with creamy sauce and melted cheese (sometimes breadcrumbed)

Eaglescliffe (female, 1962, C1442/00083) *a local regional dish is a parmo I think loosely based on Italian food which is made from pork with a cheese sauce probably parmo coming from the word parmesan*

UD (2004) 'Teesside'

PEELY-WALLY adj. pale, sickly, feeble

London (female, 1963, C1442/00876) *peely-wally I think comes from India originally and it means pale person peely being yellow I think in Hindi and wally meaning person my grandmother used to use it if you looked at all unwell she'd say 'oh you look peely-wally'*

North Scotland (male, 1959, C1442/01156) *peely-wally I think is a North of Scotland word and it means somebody who looks pale insipid lacking in colour and one of the things*

I like about northern words is that many of the words actually sound like they mean peely-wally sounds to me exactly as it means if you saw somebody who had come through the long winter in Scotland without much sunshine and they looked very white and insipid or slightly poorly you'd say 'my goodness you're looking very peely-wally'

OED (1832) 'originally and chiefly Scottish'

cf. FEMMER, FUSHIONLESS, SHILPIT

PEGGLE n. cowslip

Luton (female, 1949, C1442/00829) *when I was young my mum used to call cowslips peggles and she was from Essex so I think it's an Essex word for cowslips*

OED (1526) *paigle* 'English regional (chiefly east) and Welsh English (Pembrokeshire)'; EDD records *peggle* as localised spelling variant

PENG adj. physically attractive

British Asian (female, 1993, C1442/00219) *peng means attractive*

India (male, 1981, C1442/00012) *peng is a word that comes from India it means nice*

London (male, 1966, C1442/00036) *peng from penguin meaning fit or attractive that's a good one*

London (female, 1993, C1442/00398) *some people in London use for attractive peng*

London (male, 1994, C1442/01280) *there's a word meaning attractive I've no idea where it came from my friends started saying it one day and so if you see a girl that's good-looking or attractive you go 'she's really peng'*

London (female, 1996, C1442/01123) *peng means attractive*

Nottingham (male, 1991, C1442/00951) *when we say attractive from Nottingham we usually say 'she's a bit peng' or if you've just had a meal you might say 'oh that was peng' or if you think something sounds good you say 'oh that sounds peng'*

Nottingham (female, 1993, C1442/00823) *we use words like peng which means they're attractive to you*

DCS [c. 2000] 'originally Jamaican'

cf. BOOM-TING, BUFF (TING), HOT, TICK

PENK vb. to people-watch, pass time in idle observation of others

Surrey (female, 1988, C1442/02423) *we use the word penking this means not being nosy but wandering around say a campsite when you're camping and just looking at what other people are doing just generally people watching but not in a stalker-y way it started in my grandma's generation and just passed on down but I don't know anybody else who uses it or where it's from it but it's a very useful word*

PIKELET n. crumpet, muffin

Rotherham (female, 1938, C1442/00368) *crumpet we would say pikelet it's the same thing*

OED (1771) 'English regional (chiefly north and midlands)'

IStock Photo

PINGLE vb. to pick at food, eat fussily

Norfolk (male, 1947, C1442/02003) *pingle to eat pickily squeamishly or reluctantly*

OED (1600) 'English regional (chiefly north)'

PITCH vb. (of snow) to settle on ground

West Country (female, 1944, C1442/01150) *we use the word pitch in the West Country when we mean that the snow is sticking to the ground nobody else seems to understand it but we all know what we're talking about*

EDD *petch* Somerset

PLANK n. fool (used affectionately)

Enfield (female, 1984, C1442/02655) *plank used to describe something that's a bit stupid or thick so if somebody does something really silly like forget their keys you say 'oh you plank' essentially it means like a plank of wood quite thick and a little bit useless*

OED (1981) 'colloquial' derived from *thick as two planks* (1974)

cf. BARMPOT, BUMBLEKLUTZ, BUMBOCLOT, DAFT/SOPPY HAPORTH, EEJIT, GIMP, NUMPTY, TWONK, WAZZOCK, WUMPERT

PLAY POP vb. to express one's anger, react furiously

Yorkshire (female, 1952, C1442/00759) *a phrase from Yorkshire that's still used but used to be used much more when I was younger to play pop which is to be cross to make a fuss to rant and rave a bit I've never quite known what it means but it always makes me smile*

EDD *there'll be hell to pop* West Yorkshire

PLODGE vb. to paddle, wade, trudge through e.g. mud, slush, water

Newcastle upon Tyne (female, 1944, C1442/01621) *plodge to put your feet into water usually sea-water we usually say 'I'm ganning plodging' meaning you're going to put your feet in the water down at Cullercoats*

Sunderland (male, C1442/01617) *plodging in the clarts means paddling in mud I was brought up in Sunderland and I guess that's where it comes from*

OED (1825) 'chiefly Scottish and English regional (north)'

POT n. plaster cast

West Yorkshire (female, 1952, C1442/02641) *we use the word pot for a plaster cast when somebody's broken their leg and you say 'oh he broke his leg and he had a pot put on' and it causes so much confusion because it's a phrase that people don't use in other areas of the north*

PUCKATERRY n. muddle, confusion

Norwich (male, 1947, C1442/02103) *puckaterry Norfolk word for being in a muddle and getting things wrong*

EDD *pucker* [= 'state of confusion, agitation vexation']; *Broad Norfolk* (Jonathan Mardle, 1972) *in a puckaterry*

cf. PANSHITE, TWO AND EIGHT

PUGGLE vb. to prod, poke about in e.g. hole to clear obstruction

Southern England (female, 1981, C1442/01180) *to have a puggle in something would be to have a poke about in something*

OED (1863) 'regional (chiefly south east)'

PUT THE WOOD IN THE HOLE phr. shut the door

Huddersfield (female, 1944, C1442/01952) *when anyone leaves the door open in our house someone will say 'put t' wood in th'oil' meaning put the wood in the hole and it means you've got to shut the door which is self-explanatory*

GDS (1921)

Q

QUARE adj. odd, strange

Dublin (female, 1974, C1442/01101) *quare meaning slightly strange my father used the phrase 'I bet he walks away from a quare shite' meaning a gentleman who might be a little bit unusual would inevitably have everything unusual about him including his excrement*

OED (1805) 'Irish English'

NOTES The figure of speech quoted by this speaker as used by his father brings to mind the mischievous – but not overtly offensive – use of colourful language I associate with many speakers born in the early and mid-twentieth century. As a child I hardly ever heard anyone of that generation use extreme four-letter words, but terms like *bugger*, *arse* and *swine* were sprinkled liberally into any conversation and frequently used with impressive originality. The obvious delight speakers took in this kind of mildly rebellious linguistic behaviour is captured beautifully in the 1990s BBC sit-com *The Royle Family* – most notably in Jim Royle's catchphrase *my arse*. My favourite example is a scene from 1999 (Series 2, Episode 3) when Barbara, inspired by watching Laurence Llewelyn-Bowen presenting *Changing Rooms*, wonders aloud whether she might stencil the kitchen units, to which Jim gleefully responds *stencil my arse*. My father (born in Castleford in 1934) has a number of similarly imaginative ways of expressing his opinion, including a metaphor he uses to express displeasure or frustration at an infuriatingly useless object or person. A blunt knife might prompt the observation *I've shat sharper knives than this*, and following an uninspiring evening in front of the TV we might be informed *I've shat better programmes than that*. His *stencil my arse* moment, though, came during a particularly unimpressive England performance at the 1980 European Football Championships when he proclaimed he'd *shat better left backs than Mick Mills*. They used to say if ever England needed a fast bowler they could whistle for one down a mine in Yorkshire. During the 1980s England football managers could have solved obvious deficiencies in the international squad by visiting a certain toilet in Yorkshire.

QUELCH vb. quiche, flan

East Midlands (female, 1961, C1442/01028) *my grandma who was broad Cornish used to refer to quiche as quelch and we always now call quiche quelch in our family*

R

RATCH vb. to rummage about

Cumbria (male, 1942, C1442/00513) *ratching around means scrabbling about in various bits and pieces*

Yorkshire (female, 1962, C1442/01588) *a phrase that I picked up when I lived in Carlisle for a long time was to ratch in a cupboard or have a rummage about to find something and it is a word that I use in my everyday language and a lot of friends say to me 'what on earth are you talking about?'*

OED (1818) 'English regional (north) and Scotland'

cf. GUDDLE

REDD vb. to clear away

Newcastle upon Tyne (female, 1931, C1442/01660) *to redd the table means to clear the table now that's a Geordie word*

OED (1479) 'Irish, Scottish and English regional (north and midlands)'

cf. SIDE

RIDONKULOUS adj. ridiculous, outrageous, absurd

Edinburgh (female, 1987, C1442/00874) *it's a derivative from ridiculous and an example of how it would be used is 'that hat is ridonkulous'*

DCS 'American'

cf. FANTABULOUS

RIVE vb. to tear, tug, pull vociferously

Newcastle upon Tyne (female, 1931, C1442/01660) *to tear paper we say rive it up*

OED (1400) 'Scottish and English regional (north)'

RONKING adj. smelly, disgusting

Black Country (female, 1989, C1442/00907) *if something smells bad in the Black Country then you would say 'it's ronking' which I think is funny for a word that smells*

OED *rank* (1479); EDD records *ronk* as localised spelling variant

cf. MINGING

ROUND THE WREKIN phr. the long way round

Birmingham (female, 1978, C1442/02116) *this is a Black Country word that basically means you're going around the back way to get somewhere so when me and my dad are driving along in the car I will say 'oh dad you're not going round the Wrekin are you?' and his reply is normally 'yes' because he hates going on the direct route he likes to go literally round the Wrekin which is round all the back roads*

UD (2009)

ROVE n. scab

East Anglia (female, 1962, C1442/01916) *if you've fallen down and hurt your knee the crusty bit that forms on top of the wound we would call a rove*

OED (1475) 'English regional (Suffolk)'

ROWIE n. bread roll

Aberdeen (female, 1961, C1442/00448) *it's rowie in Aberdeen for a roll*

DSL (1656) 'modern Scots dialect'

cf. COB, STOTTY

S

SAND-SHOE n. plimsoll, child's soft shoe worn for PE

Somerset (female, 1960, C1442/01598) *in our house we call plimsolls daps which comes from Somerset but the rest of the family who come from the North East of England always refer to them as sand-shoes*

OED (1858)

cf. DAP

SCOP vb. to throw

Cumbria (male, 1947, C1442/02682) *scop is a word for throw used quite extensively in West Cumbria I'm not sure whether it's used in any other part of the country so 'scop that ball over here' is the same as saying 'throw that ball over here'*

EDD *scop* Cumberland

SCRUMP vb. to steal (esp. apples from orchard)

Chesterfield (female, 1989, C1442/00457) *I've always quite liked the word scrumping it means to steal apples really but where I come from it can mean to steal anything out of a field I just like the way it sounds I think it's quite an old word because my grandfather seems to know it I tend to use it more with my parents than with my friends*

OED (1866) 'dialect or slang'

SERI-FOR-REALLY phr. serious, genuine

Scotland (female, 1957, C1442/01021) *are you seri-for-really means are you serious or really it comes from the Catherine Tate Show I think if you're really shocked and you don't believe what someone says you go 'are you seri-for-really' it's quite commonly used in my year at school and it's quite amusing I think personally*

SHAMMOCKY adj. scruffy

Norfolk (female, 1943, C1442/02115) *my mum used to say to me when I'd not got my scarf on properly 'come you here you look real shammocky' and shammocky meant scruffy and untidy and 'let me sort out your scarf out and make you look a bit better'*

OED (1812) *shammocking* [= 'slovenly, untidy']

SHANK vb. to stab

London (female, C1442/00398) *in London stab would be shank*

NPD (1955) 'US'

SHILPIT adj. weak, sickly-looking, feeble

Glasgow (female, 1972, C1442/01025) *an interesting word from Glasgow possibly the whole of Scotland is the word shilpit it means kind of thin and undernourished and shifty all three things at once I don't know any word like that in mainstream English*

DSL (1812) 'General Scots'

FEMMER, FUSHIONLESS, PEELY-WALLY

SHORT WEEKENDS n. trousers which are too short

Kimberley, Nottinghamshire (male, 1986, C1442/01748) *short weekends might be quite distinctive to where I went to school or north Nottingham it means that your trousers are too short for you*

UD (2007)

SHUBBS n. Party

London (male, 1994, C1442/00080) *shubbs means a party so you say to someone 'I'm going to a shubbs tonight'*

DCS (2000) 'Caribbean'

IStock Photo

SHUNTLER n. Bauble

Chesterfield (male, 1968, C1442/00852) *shuntler I've always wondered if it's a real word because it's one that my mum uses for Christmas tree decorations baubles but my dad always insisted it wasn't a real word it was one that she'd made up and I've never come across anyone else that uses that word and I'd be really interested to know if it was something she made up which she insists it's not*

IStock Photo

EDD *shuntle* [= 'to shine'] Yorkshire and Derbyshire

NOTES This is not a term I have encountered previously but it has been taken up with great enthusiasm at home. Our three children get so excited in the run-up to decorating the Christmas tree that we nicknamed them 'the tinsel kid', 'the Christmas fairy' and 'the shuntler'. Unfortunately this recently led to some confusion as my daughter used *schuntler* at school thinking it was German for 'bauble'.

SICK adj. great, excellent

Manchester (female, 1987, C1442/01917) *sometimes with my friends I say 'that's sick' meaning that's extremely good I've got a feeling it comes from Afro-Caribbean influences British Asian influences as well that's where I seem to hear it the most*

West Midlands (female, C1442/01332) *one of the most common phrases I use is sick for something really good it's extremely common between me and my mates we would say 'how was the gig last night' 'oh it was sick'*

OED (1983) 'slang, esp. skateboarding and surfing'

cf. BOSS, CANNY, CHAMPION, CUSHTY, LUSH, MINT, NANG, WICK

NOTES This use of *sick* follows the pattern of several slang terms in which the conventional meaning is inverted by speakers who subsequently use it as an all-purpose term of approval. The OED records a similar process with *wicked* from the 1920s and *bad* from the 1950s onwards, for example. Taken out of context this can, of course, lead to confusion between the generations as illustrated by a text message I recently received from my daughter. Having just seen one of her favourite bands at Reading Festival she texted: *Peace just finished! fifth row! was sick!* I chose to interpret this as good news.

SIDE vb. to clear away

Lancashire (female, 1935, C1442/01949) *I think the way we use set and side a table is quite interesting because when I say 'let's side the table' nobody outside Lancashire seems to know that they lay the table and clear the table I did look up side and in the eighteenth and early nineteenth century it seems to mean tidy I had thought it meant put on the side table maybe it just means tidy away*

Yorkshire (female, 1964, C1442/00314) *we say we set the table but also we side the table I think it's from Lancashire my mother uses it so we all use it too so we side the table after we've eaten putting everything away*

OED (1848) 'dialect'

cf. REDD

SILE DOWN vb. to rain heavily

Grimsby (female, 1939, C1442/01378) *siling down raining very hard*

OED (1703) 'dialect'

IStock Photo

SKINCHIES excl. truce term guaranteeing immunity from capture in children's game

Skipton (female, 1982, C1442/00993) *the word I use is skinchies it means a bit like surrender for example if you were messing about with your siblings and one of them was tickling you and you wanted them to stop you would say 'skinchies' but I don't know where it comes from*

OED (1870) 'school slang, originally dialect'; *The Lore and Language of Schoolchildren* (Peter & Iona Opie, 1959) *skinch* North East

cf. FAINITES, SQUADSIES, SQUITSIES, THOUSIES

SKRIKE vb. to cry, shriek

Lancashire (male, 1973, C1442/01914) *from Lancashire Manchester it means mainly when a baby's crying skriking*

OED (1340) 'dialect'

cf. BLART

SLAINTE phr. cheers, good health

Northern Ireland (female, 1946, C1442/02564) *slainte is the equivalent of saying cheers whenever you have a drink from the Irish Gaelic but it would be used quite commonly in Northern Ireland*

OED (1824) 'Gaelic'

SLIZZERED adj. drunk

Norwich (male, 1993, C1442/02015) *slizzered means drunk*

DCS (c.2003) 'American'

cf. GAZEBOED, LARRUPED, MORTAL, STOCIOUS

SLOUT vb. to splash, spill

Harrogate (female, 1936, C1442/01546) *slout this is a word that our milkman used when my mother was swilling the yard he said 'don't slout me missus' and that meant don't splash me with the water as she was brushing the yard I don't use it myself but I believe it's a word originating in Leeds before 1940*

OED (1726) *slouse* [= 'to wash with copious amounts of water']; EDD *slout* [= 'to bespatter'] Yorkshire

SNECK n. latch, door-catch

Newcastle upon Tyne (female, 1931, C1442/01660) *we say close the door with the sneck which is literally an old latch*

OED (1324) 'Scottish and northern dialect'

cf. SNIB

SNEET n. jibe, taunt, banter

West London (male, 1945, C1442/00117) *a word from North Staffordshire is sneet in the mining community my grandfather told me it meant a jokingly mild insult one man to show he was friendly with another would teasingly insult that person and the other person would then reciprocate by trying to come out with a better mild insult and whoever outwitted the other would be sneet*

EDD (1776) *sneest*

cf. BANTEROUS

SNIB n. latch, door-catch

London (female, 1951, C1442/02528) *snib is something to do with a lock on a door I'm not sure if it's the little bit that sticks out that the handle controls or it's the bit that holds the lock in when you've temporarily disabled the lock I think it's that because my mum from the Isle of Wight used to say 'put the door on the snib' and that meant leaving the front door lock unlocked so you could get back in without a key I think this is an Isle of Wight word but I did hear someone from Surrey using it quite recently but that's the only other time I've ever heard anyone use it*

OED (1825) 'chiefly Scottish'

cf. SNECK

SNICKET n. alleyway

Leeds (male, 1986, C1442/00521) *snicket it's an alleyway comes from West Yorkshire probably Leeds 'I'm going down the snicket to t' shops' and stuff like that we used to play in t' snicket as kids*

OED (1898) 'northern dialect'

cf. BACK-JIGGER, GENNEL, GINNEL, JITTY, TWITCHEL, TWITTEN

SOPPY HA'PORTH n. fool (used affectionately)

Bedfordshire (female, 1977, C1442/01051) *soppy ha'porth it's a word that my grandfather used to use when I was a little girl he was from the East End of London he lived in Poplar and he would use that word with me if I tried to be too affectionate he would get embarrassed and say 'get out of it you soppy ha'porth' which always makes me think of him*

GDS (1977); GDS (1950) *soft ha'porth*

cf. BARMPOT, BUMBLEKLUTZ, BUMBOCLOT, DAFT HA'PORTH, EEJIT, GIMP, NUMPTY, PLANK, TWONK, WAZZOCK, WUMPERT

SPETCH n. sticking plaster

Yorkshire (female, 1936, C1442/01544) *the word spetch means a sticking plaster that you put over a cut I think it did originate from spit if you hurt yourself you spit on it and rub the spit in because it's got healing properties*

OED (1828) *spetch* [= 'patch of cloth']; EDD *spetch* [= 'plaster']

SPOGGY n. chewing gum

Grimsby (female, 1985, C1442/01312) *when I first went to university I asked someone if they wanted a spoggy and they didn't have any idea what I was talking about I still ask people at work whether they want a spoggy and now most of them have learnt that that means chewing gum*

IStock Photo

UD (2004) 'Grimsby and surrounding areas'; DCS *spogs* [= 'sweets'] 'schoolchildren's term in north'

SPUGGY n. sparrow

Coventry (female, 1953, C1442/02492) *I use spuggy for sparrow I have got no idea where it comes from*

EDD Warwickshire

SQUADSIES excl. truce term guaranteeing immunity from capture in children's game

Leicester (male, 1993, C1442/01487) *when you're playing tig or tag you say 'squadsies' which means you cannot get tug or tigged it's like a safe base sort of thing*

The Lore and Language of Schoolchildren (Peter & Iona Opie, 1959) *squidsies* Lincolnshire

cf. FAINITES, SKINCHIES, SQUITSIES, THOUSIES

SQUIRGLE n. sausage

Maidenhead (female, 1961, C1442/00187) *squirgle it was used by my father-in-law it means sausages I don't know where it comes from*

SQUITSIES excl. truce term guaranteeing immunity from capture in children's game

Chelmsford (male, 1970, C1442/01198) *if at school you were going to be immune squitsies crossing your fingers and saying you couldn't be got I know that's different in lots of different schools*

The Lore and Language of Schoolchildren (Peter & Iona Opie, 1959) *squits* Lincolnshire

cf. FAINITES, SKINCHIES, SQUADSIES, THOUSIES

STARVE vb. to perish, freeze

Cumbria (male, 1942, C1442/00513) *starved doesn't mean short of food but means cold*

OED (1586) 'now chiefly dialect and poetic'

STOCIOUS adj. drunk

Scotland (female, 1948, C1442/02494) *for drunk stocious*

OED (1937) 'slang (chiefly Anglo-Irish)'

cf. GAZEBOED, LARRUPED, MORTAL, SLIZZERED

STOTTY (CAKE) n. bread roll

Ashington (female, 1955, C1442/01340) *one of the words I would use which one of me friends the other day found very amusing was gully for knife usually a big knife like a bread knife as in 'pass us the gully so I can cut the stotty'*

Eaglescliffe (female, 1962, C1442/00083) *from Teesside there are a couple of phrases that I see around and use one is stotty for a bread bun*

OED (1971) 'northern dialect'

cf. COB, ROWIE

STRAMASH n. uproar, row

Scotland (female, 1957, C1442/01021) *in Scotland people used to say when something was a big mess or a lot of trouble it was a stramash I think that was the Italian community in Glasgow from the Italian word stramazzo which means a big mess*

OED (1821) 'chiefly Scottish'

SUCKER n. ice lollipop

Nottingham (female, 1947, C1442/01076) *a sucker was an ice lolly and I thought everybody called them that until I moved away from home*

OED (1823) *sucker* [= 'lollipop']; *Ey Up Mi Duck!* (Richard Scollins & John Titford, 1976) *sucker* [= 'ice lolly']; VOICES Nottingham (C1190/26/05) *we used to call it a sucker when we were young 'mum can I have a sucker'*

SUMMAT n. something

Hull (female, 1998, C1442/00590) *me mam it means your mum or summat like that*

OED (1230) *somewhat* [= 'something'] 'archaic or dialect'; NPD (1984) *summat* 'phonetic slovening'

SWITHER vb. to be undecided, hesitate

Scotland (male, 1986, C1442/02493) *to swither meaning to have difficulty deciding between two options so 'I'm swithering between the brownie and the ice cream sundae'*

OED (1535) 'Scottish and dialect'

T

TARA A BIT excl. good-bye

Birmingham (female, 1974, C1442/00813) *my husband particularly when he's talking to his family who are from Birmingham when he finishes a conversation rather than saying bye or see you soon he'll say tara a bit and it always amuses me because he only really uses it when he's talking to other people from Birmingham*

OED *tara* (1958) 'colloquial (mainly northern) alteration of *ta-ta* (1823); *The Black Country Dialect: a Modern Linguistic Analysis* (Ed Conduit, 2007) *tara a bit*

TATERS adj. cold, chilly

London (male, 1964, C1442/01376) *'it's taters outside' means it's very cold weather*

NPD (1936) 'rhyming slang for *taters* [= 'potatoes'] *in the mould'*

cf. DERBY (ROAD), NITHERED, PARKY, THANDA

TATTER n. walk (with dog)

Shropshire (female, 1993, C1442/02764) *tatters means walk we use it when we're talking about taking the dogs for a walk so 'are we gonna take the dogs for tatters' I've no idea where it comes from*

OED (1825) *tatter* [= 'to move, bestir oneself'] 'dialect'

TEETERMATORTER n. see-saw

Norfolk (female, 1953, C1442/02091) *teetermatorter is a Norfolk word for a see-saw*

EDD Suffolk

THANDA adj. cold

Midlands (male, 1993, C1442/01410) *thanda which means cold I think it's from Punjabi*

The Panjabi Dictionary (Maya Singh, 1895) *thanda* [= 'cold']

cf. DERBY (ROAD), NITHERED, TATERS, PARKY

NOTES Many first and second-generation children of immigrant communities are acutely aware of their bilingual status. Such speakers demonstrate a fascinating tendency to code-switch – that is they can alternate between different languages as circumstance dictates, often within the same utterance. In most cases this process is subconscious and simply indicative of the fact a speaker does not know the appropriate word in one of the languages they speak or that one language has a particular expression that captures the intended meaning more precisely. In other cases, switching between languages is a more conscious marker of shared identity or group solidarity, such as when speakers mix English and Punjabi with Asian friends. The rise of multi-lingual, multi-ethnic communities in the UK has inevitably led to individual words from heritage languages being adopted by the wider speech community. A retired white police officer, for instance, in a VOICES recording in Oldham (C1190/04/02) also claims he uses *thanda* to refer to particularly cold weather.

At its simplest code-switching involves the use of a single word from one language in an utterance otherwise entirely framed in another language, but it can also be more complex and involve the transfer of grammatical features from one language to the vocabulary of another. A young British Asian female from Leeds, for instance, recorded the following contribution to the WordBank (C1442/01578): *I use a number of Asian words in my everyday language 'I've gunned the atta and I'll sek the rotis later' that means I've kneaded the dough and I'll cook the chapatis later on. The Panjabi Dictionary* records *gunnhna* [= 'to knead'], *atta* [= 'flour'], *sekna* [= 'to toast'] and *roti* [= 'chapati'] but what is instructive here is the way the speaker applies English grammar to Punjabi words by, for instance, adding the conventional English plural suffix <-s> to form *rotis*, the regular past tense suffix <-ed> to create *gunned* and a more typically English sounding infinitive form *sek*.

Perhaps the most widely known phenomenon attributed to British Asian code-switching is the invariant tag *innit* used in statements like *I can't afford it, innit*. Tag-questions, such as *don't you, couldn't he, wasn't it* and so on are used at the end of statements to confirm whether a listener has understood or to invite them to confirm or dispute something that has just been said. In Standard English a tag-question refers back to the subject of the previous clause and thus this statement would more conventionally be rendered *I can't afford it, can I*. The all-purpose tag-question *innit* is thought to derive from use among the British Asian community, as it mirrors the corresponding construction in South Asian languages (think also French *n'est-ce pas* and German *nicht wahr*), although there are also similar reflexes in some traditional dialects, particularly those in the South West of England and in Wales. Whatever its origins it is certainly on the increase among young speakers throughout the UK regardless of ethnic background.

THEAVE vb. ewe prior to bearing first lamb

East Midlands (female, 1973, C1442/01242) *my father who's a sheep farmer in south Leicestershire uses the word theave to describe the sheep equivalent of a heifer so that's a ewe lamb that's growing up but hasn't yet had a lamb of its own*

OED (1465) 'local'

THOUSIES excl. truce term guaranteeing immunity from capture in children's game

Poole (female, 1993, C1442/00351) *when I was a kid we used to say the word thousies when we were playing it or tag and it would basically mean that the tagger couldn't get you because you had your fingers crossed and you'd said 'thousies' and for some reason this made you immune and I've never heard it used anywhere else*

NOTES *The Lore and Language of Schoolchildren* (Peter and Iona Opie, 1959) lists numerous regional variants for 'truce terms' – the code word used to withdraw briefly from a playground chasing game or to seek immunity from capture – including *barley* in the West Midlands, *skinch* in the North East, *kings* in Yorkshire, *cree* in South Wales and the West Country, *fainites* in the Home Counties and South East and *scribs* in Hampshire. *The Lore of the Playground* (Steve Roud, 2010)

IStock Photo

confirms continued use of many of these terms alongside more mainstream national variants such as *time out, paxies* and *freeze* and previously unrecorded local forms such as *twixies* in Essex, *jex* in Croydon and *bugsies* in Devon – but makes no mention of *thousies*. It is also worth noting how this contributor uses both *it* and *tag* to refer to a basic chase game as this, too, is known variously across the country as *it, he, tig, tag, ticky, dobby, touch, king* etc. Note also how the WordBank contributor from Leicester who supplied *squadsies* as his truce term (C1442/01487) is unsure whether the past participle of 'tig' is regular (i.e. *tigged*) or strong (i.e. *tug*). Both the Opies and Roud also report extraordinary variation in the way children continue to enjoy adapting a basic chasing and seeking concept, with local names for a variety of games including *stuck-in-the-mud, sharky, acky-one-two-three, block, chain tig, off-ground tig, forty-forty, duck duck goose, ticky scarecrow* and many more besides.

cf. FAINITES, SKINCHIES, SQUADSIES, SQUITSIES

THRAWN adj. contrary, wilful

Scotland (female, 1942, C1442/00450) *as a child my mother was always telling me that I was a thrawn child it meant that I was wilful and pig-headed*

OED (1488) 'Scottish'

THRONG adj. busy

East Midlands (male, 1956, C1442/02326) *a phrase used by my in-laws in the East Midlands particularly my father-in-law who likes to say 'I'm a bit throng' when he's under a bit of pressure I'm a bit busy it's all a bit too much for me*

OED (1623) 'Scottish and northern dialect'

TICK adj. physically attractive

London (female, 1981, C1442/00646) *for the word attractive I used to use the word tick it was used a lot all over London by younger kids and I think it originates from East London but from Jamaica probably*

NPD (2003)

cf. BOOM-TING, BUFF (TING), HOT, PENG

TISS UP vb. to somersault

Leicester (female, 1957, C1442/01381) *tissing over or tissing up which means to somersault or to turn over or twist over when I was a girl we played tissing up against the wall*

NOTES I suspect this phrase might reflect a phonological process in which the word *twist* is interpreted as *tiss* as there is considerable evidence in the SED (especially in the Midlands) of words ending in <-st> followed by a verbal or noun plural suffix <-s> pronounced locally as '-siz' – e.g. *nests* as 'nessies' or *posts* as 'powsies'. I remember my granddad (born in Saltley in 1896) always telling us to put our *vessies* [= 'vests'] on in winter, for instance, or talking about having a cough on his *chessy* [= 'chest']. I think it is possible that this speaker and her peers in childhood interpreted the third-person form of the verb *twists* [pronounced locally as 't(w) issies'] as having an infinitive *t(w)iss*, from which you can see how *t(w)issing up*, *t(w)issing over* might refer to doing handstands or somersaults against a wall.

cf. GAMBOL

TONKY adj. snobby, stuck-up

Birmingham (female, 1950, C1442/00938) *I use the word tonky and it means posh and a bit arrogant and I would use it in saying 'they were being very tonky' with some criticism in my voice I don't know where it comes from I've used it since I was at least in my twenties when I was then living in London so I don't know if it's from London or Birmingham*

TRANKLEMENTS n. ornaments, trinkets, bits and bobs

Cradley Heath (female, 1961, C1442/01205) *my mother used to use the word tranklements by which she meant ornaments bits and pieces*

OED (1586) *trinklements* 'dialect'; EDD *trankliments* North and Midlands; VOICES Dudley (C1190/05/02) *filling the space with tranklements*

cf. BITS AND BATS

TRUE DAT excl. retort used to express approval or agreement

Anglesey (female, 1998, C1442/00518) *when we agree with something with our group of friends we go 'true dat' it means that's true and it's something that we always use*

GDS (1997)

TWAG vb. to play truant

Hull (female, 1963, C1442/00592) *in Hull we use to twag which means to play truant*

Hull (male, 1990, C1442/01017) *I always used to find the word twagging or the verb to twag very funny because it means to play truant I think it's only really used in Hull or in the surrounding area*

East Riding (male, 1938, C1442/00135) *the word we use in Yorkshire for truant is to play twag usually referring to schools when you take a day off from school you play twag what's called twagging*

OED (1861) *play (the) wag*; EDD *twag* Lincolnshire and East Yorkshire

cf. MITCH, WAG

NOTES *The Lore and Language of Schoolchildren* (Peter and Iona Opie, 1959) lists numerous regional variants for 'to play truant' including *jigging* in the North West, *jouking* in parts of Scotland, *sagging* in Merseyside, *nicking off* in the North East, *mitching* in Wales and the West Country and *twagging* in East Yorkshire. The fact *play the wag* is recorded in earlier sources suggests the possibility that as this will have been widely pronounced *play t'wag* in Yorkshire it might subsequently have been re-interpreted locally as *twag*. The VOICES survey also confirms continued use of these terms alongside more mainstream national variants like *playing hookey*, *bunking off* and *skiving* and previously unrecorded local forms such as *dolling off* in Sunderland. The study also unearthed newer slang forms such as *blagging it* and *macking* or *maccy-D'ing it* [i.e. 'absconding to McDonald's'] and variants used by particular speech communities – many British Caribbeans, for instance, use *liming* while a group of settled travellers suggested *jel off* [= Anglo-Romani for 'to go away'].

TWITCHEL n. alleyway

Nottingham (female, 1947, C1442/01076) *alleyway between two houses we used to go through the twitchel to get from one place to another*

Nottingham (female, 1980, C1442/01333) *I've no idea where this comes from but I've always called a little alleyway a twitchel*

Nottinghamshire (male, 1944, C1442/00295) *twitchel which means the footpath between houses and in Leicester that footpath is referred to as a jitty or a jetty*

OED (1435) 'dialect'

cf. BACK-JIGGER, GENNEL, GINNEL, JITTY, SNICKET, TWITTEN

TWITTEN n. alleyway

Sussex (female, 1963, C1442/01201) *twitten means a very small alleyway between two streets I think it's just a Sussex word but people there use it a lot*

OED (1798) 'Sussex dialect'

cf. BACK-JIGGER, GENNEL, GINNEL, JITTY, SNICKET, TWITTEN

TWO AND EIGHT n. state (of agitation/panic)

Mile End (male, 1949, C1442/00972) *I think I've picked up and sometimes use odd rhyming slang like in a right two and eight*

OED (1938) 'rhyming slang'

cf. PANSHITE, PUCKATERRY

TWONK n. fool (used affectionately)

Birmingham (female, 1981, C1442/01521) *twonk meaning stupid*

OED (1983) 'colloquial'

cf. BARMPOT, BUMBLEKLUTZ, BUMBOCLOT, DAFT/SOPPY HA'PORTH, EEJIT, GIMP, NUMPTY, PLANK, WAZZOCK, WUMPERT

U

UP THE DANCERS phr. go upstairs, go to bed

Leeds (female, 1981, C1442/00659) *this is an expression my mother uses and her mother used it with her too it means to go upstairs we'd use it at bedtime when the children don't wanna go to bed but they need to so mum'd be 'come on up the dancers' it's one of the distinct expressions I've never heard anyone else use but I expect I'll say it to my own children I said it once to my nephew when he was being a bit naughty and it was bedtime so I guess it's ingrained*

OED (1667) 'slang'; VOICES Salford (C1190/04/05) *up the dancers*

V

VINE n. lead pencil

Newcastle upon Tyne (female, 1931, C1442/01660) *a vine is an old Viking word for a pencil they left messages on boulders with this vine that darkened when the air got to it*

EDD (1896)

W

WABBIT adj. exhausted, tired out

Aberdeen (female, C1442/01834) *wabbit means exhausted and I have never found another word to substitute for it*

OED (1895)

cf. CASSENED, FANNAKAPANNED, JIGGERED

WAG (HOP THE) vb. to play truant

Birmingham (female, 1977, C1442/00057) *when I was growing up in Birmingham we used to say wag school for playing truant which you don't hear where I live in Wales*

Blackpool (female, C1442/01907) *playing truant where I'm from in Blackpool we always used to call it wagging it or wagging school*

London (male, 1954, C1442/01464) *my mother and father both used the expression hopping the wag for playing truanting from school in the 1930s*

Sheffield (female, 1979, C1442/01564) *one phrase I'm curious about is wagging for playing truant for example 'she wagged school today' or 'are we wagging school on Friday to go shopping' I'd use it in that context I picked that phrase up when I was a teenager in Sheffield in the 90s I'm not sure what it means and where it's come from it's just this random phrase that I still use today*

OED (1847) 'slang'

cf. MITCH, TWAG

WAR NOR WORSE adj. very bad, awful

Holmfirth (female, C1442/01757) *a phrase that particularly me dad used to use is war nor worse which means worse than worse and I always found that one strange 'cause it's worse and worse it's the same word but to say it war and worse in the same phrase so war nor worse*

OED (1300) *war* [= 'worse'] 'Scots and northern dialect'; OED (1478) *nor* [= 'than'] 'Scots, Irish and English regional'

WATER BEWITCHED n. very weak tea

Scarborough (male, 1975, C1442/01786) *if you're given a weak cup of tea my dad always used to complain and I still do it without thinking by saying 'it's like water bewitched' which means it's just water with a slight bewitching so with a slight taste it's not a good thing it's a bad thing a weak cup of tea*

OED (1678) 'colloquial'

WAZZOCK n. fool (used affectionately)

North Midlands (female, 1979, C1442/00306) *wazzock as in 'you great big wazzock' I think it's possibly a Geordie word certainly northern it means a big lummox of a lad a big oaf a lug and it's quite affectionate it's not an unpleasant word I might call my son it in a teasing way it wouldn't be too insulting*

Yorkshire (female, 1962, C1442/01214) *one that springs to mind is wazzock as in 'you daft wazzock' this is a word I got from my grandma who was from Manchester it's like idiot but it's a softer version it's not quite so insulting it's an affectionate way of telling somebody off so I'll still say 'you daft wazzock' and people look at me strangely 'cause they've never heard it before*

OED (1976) 'British slang and regional (originally north)'

cf. BARMPOT, BUMBLEKLUTZ, BUMBOCLOT, DAFT/SOPPY HA'PORTH, EEJIT, GIMP, NUMPTY, PLANK, TWONK, WUMPERT

WELL adj. very, really

Cambridge (male, 1949, C1442/00847) *I remember in Leicester about twenty years ago they used to say 'he's well bad'*

London (female, C1442/00398) *in London they probably wouldn't say good it would be well good*

Suffolk (male, 1998, C1442/02456) *well good is something really good*

GDS (1962)

cf. MAIN, GURT

WESTON-SUPER, HAVE A vb. to have an unpleasant/difficult experience, experience a disappointing/embarrassing outcome

Leicestershire (male, 1994, C1442/01480) *you could say that someone was having a weston-super as in they were having a nightmare this has come from friends and just been made up*

UD (2003) records *weston* and *weston-super-mare* in this sense; OED (1904) *nightmare* [= 'unpleasant or bad experience, catalogue of disasters']

WHILE prep. till, until

Grimsby (female, 1950, C1442/00038) *while as in two while ten as opposed to two until ten which I believe comes from the Humber estuary and is in quite common usage there*

OED (c.1400) 'now dialect (chiefly north)'

NOTES I was a student in Leeds in the 1980s and frequently grateful that corner shops stayed open *eight while late*. In 1985 Leeds band The Sisters of Mercy released 'Nine While Nine', a song that includes the line *nine while nine I'm waiting for the train*, but even more impressive was the road sign (presumably still there) on the Otley Road in Headingley which advised drivers of the correct procedure at a filter lane for turning right: the sign read *do not turn <u>whilst</u> light is red* – presumably *while* would send completely the wrong message locally.

WIBBLES n. wrinkled skin on wet hands

London (male, 1940, C1442/01067) *when my son was little I put him in his bath and after a while in the warm water the skin on the tip of his fingers were all loose and turned into wrinkles and he called them wibbles and so in our family when we do the washing-up or whenever our hands are wet and we have crinkly finger-tips we say we've got wibbles*

WICK adj. great, excellent

South Coast (female, 1982, C1442/00495) *wick a shortened version of the word wicked meaning good we started saying it as a joke but now say it more and more and lots of people seem to say it too*

OED (1920) *wicked* [= 'great, excellent'] 'slang, originally US'; NPD (1920) *wick* [= 'great, excellent']

cf. BOSS, CANNY, CHAMPION, CUSHTY, LUSH, MINT, NANG, SICK

WUMPERT n. fool (used affectionately)

London (female, 1996, C1442/01178) *it was made up by me or my sisters it's usually said with silly wumpert so you go 'oh you silly wumpert' but usually as a joke it's not too mean and it's just a funny thing that we have*

OED (1908) *wump* 'slang (now rare)'

cf. BARMPOT, BUMBLEKLUTZ, BUMBOCLOT, DAFT/SOPPY HA'PORTH, EEJIT, GIMP, NUMPTY, PLANK, TWONK, WAZZOCK

Y

YAFFLE n. woodpecker

Yeovil (female, 1964, C1442/02760) *when I went up to university I was doing biology and lots of people up there had never heard of yaffles well yaffles is woodpeckers*

OED (1792) 'dialect'

YCH A FI excl. yuck, ugh

Swansea (female, 1988, C1442/00438) *this word means disgusting you can use it with friends or family if you find something disgusting it's Welsh but it's a slang term and it goes ych a fi*

UD (2008)

YOGURT-WEAVER n. person keen on heritage crafts/ethnic culture/New Age spirituality

South West England (female, 1974, C1442/00838) *yogurt-weaver came out of the road protest camps in the eighties nineties in England around the camp fire a yogurt-weaver is someone really into New Age spirituality and cosmic stuff and who has a dietary preference for healthy foods and inclination towards ceremony and magic rather than a practical hands-on approach which was the divide on the camps at the time so someone was said to be too much of a yogurt-weaver and tofu-welder as well*

GDS (2004)

Z

ZAYDE n. grandfather

Hackney (female, 1949, C1442/02383) *my husband is called zayde which is from the Yiddish for grandfather*

OED (1946) 'Yiddish'

cf. BUBBE

Dialect collectors

John Ray, also famous for his interest in classifying plants and animals, published in 1674 one of the first serious attempts to collate and analyse English dialect words in his *Collection of English Words*. He compiled his data from first-hand observations as a result of travelling extensively across the country. Ray divided his collection into two categories: northern and southern, a division that still dominates popular conceptions of present-day regional speech in Britain. Many entries still resonate today, such as *nesh* [= 'soft, weedy and susceptible to cold'], a word which remains a local favourite in the Midlands and North of England as the WordBank testifies.

The systematic study of English dialects gained momentum in the 19th century, culminating in the extraordinary work of Joseph Wright. Of humble Bradford origins and with no formal education, Wright nevertheless pursued a successful academic career, eventually becoming Professor of Comparative Philology at Oxford. His greatest legacy is the remarkable six-volume *English Dialect Dictionary*, which he published at his own expense between 1898 and 1905. It remains the most comprehensive account of English dialect vocabulary and influenced the major dialect surveys of the 20th century, notably the *Survey of English Dialects* and *Dictionary of American Regional English*. Like its great Victorian counterpart, the *Oxford English Dictionary*, it was a collaborative effort with readers all over the country submitting suggested entries in response to Wright's request for examples of local vocabulary. Entries were compiled from printed evidence in newspapers, books and local pamphlets and include a definition, a set of variant spellings, pronunciation, geographic distribution and citations from published sources. The entry for *nesh*, for instance, has eight sub-fields that capture subtle distinctions in meaning – e.g. (2) 'brittle, easily broken, esp. of coal' (3) 'sickly, susceptible to cold' and (6) 'timid, cowardly' – each with a list of citations and an index of counties to indicate provenance.

Slang collectors

Richard Head's *The Canting Academy*, published in 1673, is one of the earliest collections of English underworld slang. Head claimed to have learnt many of the words in London's Newgate Prison and in the preface he states his intention to present this secret language so the general public might avoid falling prey to the tricks of *the more debauched and looser sort of people*. Head's glossary of 17th-century criminal cant includes one modern-day slang term – *booz* [= 'drink']. Most, however, are unfamiliar, although *bung* [= 'purse'] has possibly re-surfaced meaning 'bribe' – particularly in the context of football.

As with dialect, interest in slang blossomed in the 19th century. Despite claims of being original, George Kent's *Modern Flash Dictionary*, published in 1835, was compiled from several earlier sources, including the *Flash Dictionary* of 1821 and Pierce Egan's 1823 edition of *A Classical Dictionary of the Vulgar Tongue*. As a boxing enthusiast, Kent aimed to record criminal cant, sporting slang and *flash phrases now in vogue* and his cheap pamphlet was aimed at young working men interested in sport, gambling and drinking. In the early 19th century, the word *flash* had several meanings: a fashionable man about town was commonly referred to as a *flash cove* and a similar meaning survives today in the phrase *flash Harry*. Kent's dictionary includes sixty categories of *prime coves* [= 'first-class rogues'], including figures we would recognise today, like *fencers* and *shoplifters*, and unfamiliar terms, such as *priggers* [= 'pickpockets'] and *spicers* [= 'highwaymen'].

Documenting modern dialect

The *Survey of English Dialects* was a ground-breaking nationwide survey of regional speech in England directed by Professor Harold Orton at the University of Leeds. From 1950 to 1961 a team of fieldworkers collected data in 313 mostly rural localities using a questionnaire containing over 1,300 items. Informants' responses were transcribed in phonetic script on a series of recording sheets and subsequently analysed by Orton and his team of researchers. Answers to every question from all 313 sites were published in several volumes between 1962 and 1971. The material continues to be used by researchers worldwide and has led to a number of dedicated publications, most notably the *Linguistic Atlas of England*, published in 1978. The fieldwork was later supplemented by a sound recording programme and most sites were re-visited to record either an original informant or a speaker with a similar profile. The sound recordings feature speakers reflecting on domestic and working life and extracts are available online at the British Library's 'Sounds' website (http://sounds.bl.uk).

A *Survey of Anglo-Welsh Dialects*, directed by David Parry at the University of Swansea, was carried out on similar principles between 1968 and 1991. Given the later date of this survey, in some cases whole interviews were tape-recorded, digital copies of which are archived at the British Library. The *Linguistic Survey of Scotland* (which also included fieldwork in Northern Ireland) differed considerably in that it sought to record both Scottish English and Gaelic. The survey began in 1949 at the University of Edinburgh and was initially based on postal questionnaires sent to primary school head teachers who were asked to find a suitable local informant to complete them. From 1955 trained fieldworkers also visited several sites and used a phonological questionnaire designed specifically to capture pronunciation features. The results of the English/Scots component of the survey were published in three volumes between 1975 and 1986.

These prestigious studies established the geographic distribution of hundreds of fascinating regional terms such as 'minute fragment of wood stuck in a finger' – *splinter* in most of the English South and Midlands, *shiver* or *sliver* in East Anglia, Lincolnshire and Sussex, *splint* in the North West, *spell*, *speel*, *spile* or *spool* in the North and *spelk* in the North East, while *spilk* was recorded in Wales and several variants, including *jag*, *risp*, *stob* and *skelf*, were documented in Scotland and Northern Ireland.

Documenting modern slang

Eric Partridge's *A Dictionary of Slang and Unconventional English*, first published in 1937, ran to eight editions by 1984 and is widely acknowledged as the definitive record of 20th-century British slang. During his lifetime Partridge published over forty works on the English language but is best remembered for his dictionary, which filled a substantial gap overlooked by more mainstream reference works, by allowing evidence from unpublished sources such as popular song, film, radio and (later) television. Part of the appeal of the earlier volumes is his inclusion of supporting notes in the form of anecdotal observation and, having served in both World Wars, he gives considerable prominence to British Forces' slang. More recently *The New Partridge Dictionary of Slang and Unconventional English* (now edited by Tom Dalzell and Terry Victor) maintains the tradition impressively, enhanced by a more conventional approach to citing sources and a broader focus to include examples of colloquial and vernacular vocabulary worldwide with an emphasis on usage since 1945.

An equally eminent figure in modern slang lexicography is Jonathon Green, who over several decades has compiled a database of slang that led in 2010 to the eponymous *Green's Dictionary of Slang*. Like Wright's dialect dictionary these three large volumes are almost entirely the work of one man and similarly impressive in scope. The dictionary defines over 100,000 words spanning five centuries and from all over the English-speaking world. Entries follow *Oxford English Dictionary* conventions and thus include dates that record earliest known usage and authenticated, fully referenced citations. In 2014 British linguist, Tony Thorne, published the fourth edition of his *Dictionary of Contemporary Slang*, which pays particular attention to youth slang. Its main distinguishing feature is the priority given to spoken forms drawn from the author's own observations, conversations with students, evidence provided by internet chat rooms and from contributions submitted to the Slang Archive at King's College London. To ensure only authentic examples are accepted entries have to be corroborated by more than one source.

Together these publications constitute an impressive inventory of recent and present-day British slang from traditional nicknames for common surnames such as *Smudger* [= 'Smith'], *Nobby* [= 'Clark(e)'] and *Dusty* [= 'Miller'] and well-established rhyming slang like *butcher's* [= butcher's hook, i.e. 'look'], *barnet* [= Barnet Fair, i.e. 'hair'] and *on my tod* [= Tod Sloan, i.e. 'on my own'] to examples of British Caribbean and British Asian terms like *swear down* [= 'honestly, genuinely'], *butters* [= 'ugly'] and *desi* [= 'traditional Indian' as used pejoratively by young British Asians more assimilated into western culture and fashion] and evidence of our continued fascination with the playful possibilities of rhyming slang as confirmed by *britneys* [= Britney Spears, i.e. 'beers'], *chalfonts* [= Chalfont St Giles, i.e. 'piles/haemorrhoids'] and *frank* [= Frank Zappa, i.e. 'TV remote control'].

Documenting modern nonce-words

If capturing authentic examples of dialect and slang is challenging, then monitoring nonce-words is almost impossible. Evidence is hard to find and even harder to evaluate as it is by its nature restricted to private use and typically short-lived. There have been occasional attempts to publish glossaries, often in the form of humorous proposals for new words for everyday phenomena for which no alternative exists. The *Not 1982 Annual*, for instance, written by scriptwriters of the BBC comedy sketch show *Not the Nine O'clock News*, proposed a set of terms, including *fot* [= 'sound made by breaking seal on new jar of coffee'], *ely* [= 'first inkling that something may have gone wrong'] and *acquadextrous* [= 'ability to turn bath taps on and off using feet']. This was followed by a series of publications starting in 1983 with *The Meaning of Liff: The original dictionary of things there should be words for* and later *Afterliff* and *The Deeper Meaning of Liff*, in which the authors assigned imaginative definitions to British place names, including *didcot* [= 'small geometric shape which ticket inspector clips out of rail or bus ticket'], *spofforth* [= 'to tidy up room before cleaning lady arrives'] and *yarmouth* [= 'to shout increasingly loudly at foreigners to make oneself understood'].

Crowd-sourcing present-day vernacular forms

The advent of the World Wide Web and access to unprecedented amounts of linguistic data and two-way communication with speakers presents both a challenge and an opportunity to linguists. In the context of vernacular speech – particularly British English vernacular speech – the following noteworthy initiatives show how the internet can be harnessed not only to track language use, but also to engage the public in collaborative language research and documentation.

In 2004–5 the BBC instigated a multi-platform survey, 'Voices', to create a snapshot of the linguistic landscape of the UK at the start of the 21st century. Members of the public were invited to complete an online survey by submitting the words they used for a set of everyday notions, such as 'tired', 'to play truant' and 'toilet'. Participants provided brief biographical details – age, gender, ethnicity, geographical background, education, occupation etc. – so that researchers could subsequently analyse the data to establish geographical and/or social factors that might influence individual preferences for particular variants. In tandem with the online survey, BBC Local and Nations Radio recorded 312 group conversations with over a thousand people from all walks of life talking about the same forty prompt words, and discussing attitudes to the accents and dialects they encountered in their daily lives. Conducted according to a methodology developed by researchers at the University of Leeds, 'BBC Voices' constitutes the first co-ordinated attempt to record popular speech across the whole of the UK. The result is a huge database of present-day lexical variation and a substantial audio archive, the 'BBC Voices Recordings', available at the British Library 'Sounds' website. A brief glance at a subset of variants elicited for 'attractive' hints at the extraordinary diversity of contemporary English in the UK: conventional terms exhibiting varying degrees of formality like *handsome, beautiful, stunning* and *gorgeous*; phrases that give clues to a speaker's age like *buff, mint, fit* and *crumpet*; local forms like *bobby-dazzler, bonny, stoater* and *lush*; and evidence of the contribution of recently arrived speech communities in phrases like *pretty-pretty, stoosh* [= Caribbean English for 'stylish'], *sohani* [= Punjabi for 'beautiful, pleasing'] and *peng*.

A more modest survey was conducted in 2008 by the 'English Project', a group of academics and enthusiasts affiliated to the University of Winchester, who encouraged members of the public to submit family words and examples of idiolectal language to create a database of what they called kitchen table lingo. We have all probably been disappointed to discover that a word we thought a relative or friend had invented is in fact more widely known, and the book confirms how tricky it is to penetrate and evaluate language restricted to individual families and close friendship groups. On closer inspection several entries are actually examples of living dialect previously recorded in reliable dictionaries, such as *boking* [= 'to retch, vomit'], which has a long provenance in Scottish and northern dialects; *yampy* [= 'foolish, daft'], a common term in the Black Country; *chobble* [= 'to gobble, eat greedily'], listed in the *English Dialect Dictionary* as Warwickshire dialect; *juckler* [= dog], presumably derived from the Anglo-Romani word *jukkel* [= 'dog']; and *it's black over Bill's/Will's mother*, a well-known saying in the East Midlands and elsewhere if rain is imminent. Likewise numerous items are slang terms used (inter)nationally and reported in other compilations such as *boom-ting* [= British Caribbean youth slang for 'attractive person'], *bizzle* [= 'bit' modified by the suffix <-izzle> commonly used in hip-hop, e.g. *drizzle* meaning 'drink' or *fo' shizzle* meaning 'for sure'], *testiculate* [= 'to wave one's arms about while talking bollocks'] and, intriguingly, *pfot* [= 'to open new jar of coffee' – cf. *fot* in the *Not 1982 Annual*]. Nonetheless *Kitchen Table Lingo* includes several words and phrases that are indisputably genuine neologisms and is a worthy celebration of our individual and shared linguistic creativity, showcasing wonderful terms like *pook* [= 'round piece of jigsaw that fits into hole of adjacent piece'], *shistlepot* [= 'thingummyjig'], *humsecker* [= 'double-ended oven glove'] and a seemingly endless list of words for 'TV remote control' including *cajunka, commander, phaser, remy, spurgler* and *twidger*.

Finally, in many ways the recent proliferation of online dictionaries featuring user-generated content mirrors the collaborative nature of 19th-century dictionary compilation: a distributed network of contributors supplying evidence of linguistic usage to a central collecting point. Unlike their print counterparts, however, editorial intervention varies (or is non-existent) and thus online glossaries have to be treated with a degree of caution regarding authenticity. Perhaps the best-known and certainly the most extensive of these online platforms is *Urban Dictionary*. Founded in 1999 by US computer science undergraduate, Aaron Peckham, the site now claims over seven-and-a-half-million 'definitions' at the time of writing (February 2014). This figure includes numerous entries that are in fact simply variant spellings and/or multiple definitions of the same word or phrase, so this should be taken into account when assessing the real size (and reliability) of the data set. Anyone can submit an entry, which is then approved by a team of voluntary editors, although criteria for inclusion are at best unclear and unlikely to be applied consistently. Entries typically include a headword or phrase, a definition expressed in free text and, in most cases, an example of usage, but because contributors include all ages and social groups, including non-native speakers, the entries can be frustratingly inconsistent and are frequently difficult to evaluate. Nonetheless this inherent weakness is also arguably one of the dictionary's strengths in that it captures nuanced usage across diverse speaker groups and allows contradictory definitions that show how speakers interpret a word differently. Above all the flexibility of an online repository such as *Urban Dictionary* with its instantaneous uploads means that new terms are captured with impressive speed.

A quick glance at entries in *Urban Dictionary* relevant to British English is both entertaining and informative. Given the lack of editorial control it is perhaps no surprise that there is a disproportionate amount of attention given to sexual practice, including offensive terms like *tesco legs* [= girl who has her legs open 24/7, i.e. 'promiscuous'] and *bobfoc* [= acronym for *body off Baywatch face off Crimewatch*, i.e. 'ugly' – a modern take on *nice legs shame about the face*, which was the title of a 1979 UK hit single by The Monks]. There is also a predictable obsession with drugs, alcohol and toilet humour with countless variants for 'drunk' such as *carpeted*, *bungalowed* and one my nineteen-year-old son recently used – *hooned*. Nonetheless there are also several entries that capture contemporary regional variation in the UK with 'new' dialect words like *spoggy* [= 'chewing gum' in Grimsby], *nerks* [= 'chips' in Yorkshire] and local pride and/or rivalry expressed in, for instance, *lobby gobbler* [= 'person from Leigh, Lancashire'], *meggie* [= 'person from Cleethorpes, Lincolnshire'], *plastic scouser* [= 'person from the Wirral'] and *meader* [= pejorative term used in Bristol for 'typical Southmead youth']. There are also examples of British slang across the generations in entries like *Gordon Bennett* [= exclamation of shock or surprise], *allow* and *bun it* [= 'I can't be bothered to do that, I'm not interested'], *you get me* [= empty tag phrase corresponding to 'know what I mean'], *bricking it* [= 'extremely nervous'], *safe* [= general term of approval or agreement] and *quality* [= 'top notch, first rate, excellent']. Finally *Urban Dictionary* bears further witness to our enduring obsession with rhyming slang and offers an insight into how an essentially historic London feature remains relevant as speakers can generate modern cultural references in forms like *brad* [= Brad Pitt, i.e. 'shit' – a culturally updated alternative to *eartha* (= Eartha Kitt) that older generations will know] or reflect contemporary British society with terms like *chicken jalfrezi* [= 'crazy'].

The WordBank, then, follows in a long line of surveys and compilations that celebrate and explore English vernacular speech and offer ordinary speakers the opportunity to ensure their variety of English is celebrated. I cannot claim it is the equal of the illustrious predecessors described here but it certainly takes its inspiration from them and I hope you enjoy reading (and using) some of these words as much as I have enjoyed compiling them. Finally, special thanks to all the visitors to the Evolving English exhibition who took the time to ensure their words get the attention they deserve and to Holly Gilbert, a British Library colleague who has assisted greatly in cataloguing the WordBank.

British Library audio collections

BBC Voices Recordings. BBC, UK, rec. 2004-2005 [digital audio files] British Library, C1190. Available online at < http://sounds.bl.uk/Accents-and-dialects/BBC-Voices >.

Evolving English VoiceBank. British Library, UK, rec. 2010-2011 [digital audio files] British Library, C1442. Selected items available online at < http://sounds.bl.uk/Accents-and-dialects/Evolving-English-WordBank>.

Survey of Anglo-Welsh Dialects. Survey of Anglo-Welsh Dialects/Penhallurick, R., UK, rec. 1965-1991 [digital audio files] British Library, C1314. Selected extracts available online at <http://www.bl.uk/soundsfamiliar>.

Survey of English Dialects. University of Leeds, UK, rec. 1952-1974 [digital audio files] British Library, C908. Selected extracts available online at <http://sounds.bl.uk/Accents-and-dialects/Survey-of-English-dialects>.

Voices of the UK. 2010. British Library, UK [audio CD] NSACD 74-75, 153 mins.

Multi-media references

'Allinson Bread.' 1992, (prod. co. n.k.), UK, 31 secs, [advert] http://www.tvwhirl.co.uk/tvwhirl.php?file=tesadverts/allinson1992.mp4 (accessed 21 May 2014).

Coronation Street. Granada Television, UK, (20.30), 31/03/14, ITV1, 29 mins.

'Defeat You,' *Uncle B*, Perf. N-Dubz, Prod. N-Dubz, UK. 2008. [CD: Universal Music, TV 1790382]. 02 mins 56 secs.

Downton Abbey Christmas Special 2012. Carnival Films, UK, (21.00), 25/12/12, ITV1, 92 mins.

EastEnders. BBC, UK, (20.00), 05/05/14, BBC1, 30 mins.

EastEnders. BBC, UK, (20.00), 13/05/14, BBC1, 30 mins.

EastEnders. BBC, UK, (19.30), 29/05/14, BBC1, 30 mins.

Evolving English: One Language, Many Voices. 2010 [public exhibition] London: British Library, 17/11/2010–03/04/2011.

'Fred Fannakapan,' Perf. Gracie Fields, Cond. Ray Noble, (prod, n.k.), UK. 1930. [LP: HMV, B 3595]. 03 mins 30 secs.

'From the Ritz to the Rubble,' *Whatever People Say I Am That's What I'm Not*, Perf. Arctic Monkeys, Prod. Jim Abiss/Alan Smyth, UK. 2006. [CD: Domino, WIGCD 162]. 03 mins 13 secs.

'Mardy Bum,' *Whatever People Say I Am That's What I'm Not*, Perf. Arctic Monkeys, Prod. Jim Abiss/Alan Smyth, UK. 2006. [CD: Domino, WIGCD 162]. 02 mins 55 secs.

'Nice Legs Shame About The Face,' *Bad Habits*, Perf. The Monks, Prod. Richard Hudson/John Ford/Terry Cassidy, UK. 1979. [LP: EMI, EMC 3309]. 02 mins.

'Nine While Nine,' *First and Last and Always*, Perf. Sisters of Mercy, Prod. David M. Allen, UK. 1985. [LP: Merciful Release, MR 337L]. 04 mins 12 secs.

The F Word Series 4 Episode 12. Channel 4, UK, (tx time n.k.), 29/07/08, Channel 4, 48 mins.

The Royle Family Series 2 Episode 3. BBC, UK, (22.00), 07/10/99, BBC1, 30 mins.

Bibliography

Acton, T., and Kenrick, D. 1984. *Romani Rokkeripen To-Divvus: The English Romani Dialect and its Contemporary Social, Educational and Linguistic Standing*. London: Romanestan.

Adams, D. et al. 1981. *Not 1982: Not the Nine O'clock News Rip-Off Annual*. London: Faber.

Adams, D., and Lloyd, J. 1983. *The Meaning of Liff*. London: Pan Books.

Adams, D., and Lloyd, J. 1990. *The Deeper Meaning of Liff*. London: Pan Books.

Beale, P. (ed.) 1985. *A Dictionary of Catch Phrases British and American from the Sixteenth Century to the Present Day*. London: Routledge.

Bombaugh, C.C. 1867. 'Essay to Miss Catherine Jay.' In *Gleanings from the Harvest-fields of Literature for the Curious*. Baltimore: T.N. Kurtz.

Cassidy, F.G. (ed.) 1985-2013. *Dictionary of American Regional English*. Cambridge, Mass.: Harvard University Press.

Cassidy, F.G., and Le Page, R.B. (eds.) 1980. *Dictionary of Jamaican English*. Cambridge: Cambridge University Press.

Collins English Dictionary. 2011-. Harper Collins Publishers. Online. Available HTTP: <http://www.collinsdictionary.com/>

Conduit, E. 2007. *The Black Country Dialect: A Modern Linguistic Analysis*. Stourbridge: Laghamon Publishing.

Dalzell, T., and Victor, T. 2013. *The New Partridge Dictionary of Slang and Unconventional English* 2nd edn. London: Routledge.

Dent, S. (ed.) 2012. *Brewer's Dictionary of Phrase and Fable* 19th edn. London: Brewer's.

Dictionary of the Scots Language. 2004–. Online. Available HTTP: <http://www.dsl.ac.uk/>.

Egan, P. (ed.) 1823. *Grose's Classical Dictionary of the Vulgar Tongue.* London: P. Egan.

Green, J. 2010. *Green's Dictionary of Slang.* London: Chambers.

Griffiths, W. 2011. *A Dictionary of North-East Dialect.* Newcastle: Northumbria University Press.

Grimes, D.A. 1990. *Like Dew Before the Sun: Life and Language in Northamptonshire.* Northampton: Dorothy A. Grimes.

Hawthorne, B. 2013. *Black Country Dialect.* Sheffield: Bradwell Books.

Head, R. 1673. *The Canting Academy.* London: printed by F. Leach for Mat. Drew.

Kent, G. 1835. *Modern Flash Dictionary.* London: J. Duncombe.

Kilford, V. 1981. *Shropshire Words and Dialect.* Telford: V. Kilford.

Lawrence, D.H. 1928. 'The Collier's Wife.' In *The Collected Poems of DH Lawrence.* London: Martin Secker.

Lloyd, J., and Canter, J. 2013. *Afterliff.* London: Faber and Faber.

Mather, J.Y., and Speitel, H.H. (eds.) 1975-1986. *The Linguistic Atlas of Scotland* (3 volumes). London: Croom Helm.

Opie, P., and Opie, I. 1959. *The Lore and Language of Schoolchildren.* Oxford: Oxford University Press.

Orton, H. et al (eds.) 1962-1971. *Survey of English Dialects: (A) Introduction; (B) Basic Material* (4 volumes). Leeds: E.J. Arnold.

Orton, H., Sanderson, S., and Widdowson, J.D.A. (eds.) 1978. *The Linguistic Atlas of England.* London: Croom Helm.

Oxford English Dictionary. 2010–. Oxford University Press. Online. Available HTTP: <http://www.oed.com/>.

Parry, D. 1977–1979. *Survey of Anglo-Welsh Dialects* (2 Volumes). Swansea: privately published.

Partridge, E. 1937. *A Dictionary of Slang and Unconventional English.* London: G. Routledge & Sons.

Penhallurick, R. 1991. *The Anglo-Welsh Dialects of North Wales: A Survey of Conservative Rural Spoken English in the Counties of Gwynedd and Clwyd.* Frankfurt am Mein: P. Lang.

Porter, L. 2013. 'Oxford University crewdates: a hotbed of booze, 'banter' and some casual sexism', *Daily Telegraph*, 2 April 2013.

Ray, J. 1674. *A Collection of English Words.* London: printed by H. Bruges for T. Burrell.

Rees, N. 1995. *Phrases and Sayings.* London: Bloomsbury.

Roud, S. 2010. *The Lore of the Playground: One Hundred Years of Children's Games, Rhymes and Traditions.* London: Random House.

Scollins, R., and Titford, J. 1976. *Ey Up Mi Duck! Dialect of Derbyshire and the East Midlands.* Ilkeston: Scollins & Titford.

Sillitoe, A. 1958. *Saturday Night and Sunday Morning.* London: W.H. Allen.

Singh, M. 1895. *The Panjabi Dictionary.* Lahore: Munshi Gulab Singh & Sons.

Smeeton, G. 1821. *The Flash Dictionary.* London: G. Smeeton.

The English Project. 2008. *Kitchen Table Lingo.* London: Virgin.

Thorne, T. 2014. *Dictionary of Contemporary Slang.* London: Bloomsbury.

Urban Dictionary. 1999–. Online. Available HTTP: <http://www.urbandictionary.com/>.

Widdowson, J.D.A. 1984. 'Lincolnshire Traditional Sayings and Proverbial Expressions.' In Field, N., and White, A. (eds.) *A Prospect of Lincolnshire*. Newland: F.N. Field & A.J. White.

wiktionary.org. 2002-. Online. Available HTTP: <http://www.wiktionary.org/>.

wordreference.com. 1999-. Online. Available HTTP: <http://www.wordreference.com/>.

Wright, J. 1898-1905. *English Dialect Dictionary*. London: Henry Frowde.